The *Diary* of
JOHN BRUNTON

John Brunton in 1880

1812—1899

JOHN BRUNTON'S BOOK

Being

the Memories of John Brunton, Engineer, from
a manuscript in his own hand written for his
grandchildren and now first printed

With an Introduction by

J. H. CLAPHAM

*Emeritus Professor of Economic History in
the University of Cambridge*

CAMBRIDGE
at the University Press
1939

CAMBRIDGE
UNIVERSITY PRESS

University Printing House, Cambridge CB2 8BS, United Kingdom

Cambridge University Press is part of the University of Cambridge.

It furthers the University's mission by disseminating knowledge in the pursuit of
education, learning and research at the highest international levels of excellence.

www.cambridge.org
Information on this title: www.cambridge.org/9781107511712

© Cambridge University Press 1939

First published 1939
First paperback edition 2015

A catalogue record for this publication is available from the British Library

ISBN 978-1-107-51171-2 Paperback

INTRODUCTION

Late in the Victorian era on the 7th of April
1899, John Brunton, a travelled engineer, died
aged 86. He had been in professional practice
until his seventy-eighth year. At some time in his
old age he sat down to write this story of his life.
It was meant for his grandchildren and it shows all
the kindliness and simplicity of a man who, one
feels, understood the grandfather's art: "your dear
Father" and "your dear 'Ama'" [that is, Grannie]
come into the narrative just as they should. There
are other simplicities in his character and many in
his style: "the unhappy farmer [we are in an
Indian native state in the 'fifties] was called up and
there and then his ears and nose were cut off.
Fancy such injustice and cruelty!": my Goanese
cook "was very black...but he was a Roman
Catholic and therefore a Christian". Brunton is
not merely writing in words of one syllable for the
grandchildren. He has a mind as simple and direct
as his nature is fearless, efficient and prompt. He
faces an obstructive mid-nineteenth century War
Office official and a mad wolf in India in exactly the
same way; and when he has come out of some very

tight place he observes quietly—"now was not that Providential?"

An engineer's son who had stood at Thomas Telford's knee as a child, he did not allow the influence of a gentlemanly but rough little private school to divert him to any other profession. He went through the shops in the old hard style and began his working life in an out-of-the-way Welsh colliery valley of the 'twenties, where apparently he administered justice as he pleased, and where the parson was afraid of the witch. Later he served the Stephensons on the London and Birmingham and the Manchester and Leeds. After the Stephensons, Isambard Brunel. He built a hospital above Chanak during the Crimean War and met Florence Nightingale ("a wonderful business-like woman") and Lord Lyons. He conducted hospital services himself, reading "one of Kingsley's Sermons". In his off time he did a little amateur archaeology at Troy. When the clearing up began he broke all War Office rules about the disposal of stores—Lord Lyons would accept no responsibility: "I will take all that, my Lord", said he—bought them in and sold them to the Admiralty (hospital fans to ventilate gun-boats' stokeholds), which was easy "as the several departments are ignorant of, and do not interfere with each other's transactions". He only got 5 per cent. on what he saved the War Office.

After that to the India of the Mutiny to make railways, shoot muggurs, deal with Rajahs and, being unarmed, flap his sun-topi at the mad wolf. He was dining with the Governor of Bombay when his host read a telegram which reported the fall of Delhi: "the expression on the faces of the row of Native servants fell in a most wonderful manner, I could not help noticing it. It was like shutting down Venetian blinds." The Governor sent him to bed with a "Now Brunton you may be off to Karachi as soon as you like". So he went and found a good master and colleague in Sir Bartle Frere, then Commissioner of Scinde. Besides doing his railway surveys, he cleared one station of malaria by draining a forest pool and sinking a well. On his second visit to India "we got up an Ice Company, and I was appointed Engineer to it"; he found excellent ballast for his line in the bricks of a deserted city; he acted as dispenser of quinine to whole camps and gave a blind man "some harmless drug" because he would have a dose; and he had a whole series of adventures with the Rajah who cut off ears and noses, whom he took for his first steamer trip on the Indus. Eventually he bridged the Sutlej and his bridge—like one in a Kipling story—defeated a heavy flood. And before leaving for England, in October 1865, though only a Volunteer, he wiped a Regular Colonel's eye with three bulls on the target. He must tell them this, "in spite of being considered egotistical".

After that a stupendous railway law-suit in which Brunton was chief witness: "my examination in chief extended over 2 years and my cross examination over 9 months." It was a preliminary to the less exciting work of a consulting engineer, to which he settled down in partnership with his son. He managed to have an adventure or two at collieries and slate quarries; but his story breaks off somewhere in the 'seventies when "the construction of Tramways in Towns became a popular notion... both in England and on the Continent—we had the Engineership of the Milan and Vercelli"; and we also introduced the "Brunton system" of tramway rails. "It has been adopted on the Oxford and Karachi Tramways... and has given much satisfaction." There, straddled from Karachi to Oxford, he leaves us; though we would gladly have sailed along the last quiet reaches of his English life with him, if he had launched on them and offered us a seat. For he is telling, in the authentic tone and style of the active—not the literary—nineteenth century, what we have very seldom indeed been told, a first-hand life-history of "One of our Conquerors", the versatile and matter-of-fact English engineers who left on that century its clearest, and perhaps even its most profound, identification marks.

J. H. CLAPHAM

September 1939

NOTE. *Apart from a few very brief omissions and an occasional unimportant change of pen-phrasing, the text appears as Brunton wrote it. Spelling of the names of places has therefore not been modernized, though here and there his own practice has been made more consistent.*

[The following narrative of incidents in my life I most affectionately dedicate to my seven very dear Grandchildren hoping that it may be found interesting to them and sometimes amusing; above all I pray that the perusal of it may tend to encourage them to put their simple trust in their Heavenly Father's care who in His mercy has brought me through many difficulties, and has guided and protected me through the threescore and ten years of a not uneventful career.]

I

I WAS born on the 23rd of October in the year 1812 at the house of my granduncle Mr Dickinson who with his wife were a curious old fashioned couple. They lived in a very nice house of their own on Summer Hill—Birmingham—it was then and for many years afterwards surrounded by fine old elm trees, but now all these country-like surroundings have been cut down, and the neighbourhood covered with buildings, many of them factories, having tall chimneys which are smoking from morning till night. When I went past it a few months ago, the change struck me very forcibly.

When I was born my dear Father was engaged in the Engineering management of the Butterley Iron works in Derbyshire, then the property of Mr Jessop.

Though only three years old when my Father left it, I can still recall the house in which we lived, overlooking a large reservoir of water, which turned the water wheels at the works.

We came to live in Birmingham in 1815; The first house we were in was in Regent Street, near the Sandpits, and while we lived there, two events happened which I can yet recall to my memory most vividly. The first was the occasion of the rejoicing for the battle of Waterloo in which the great Duke of Wellington won a victory over Napoleon Bonaparte the Emperor of the French, a matter of History now, and of which no doubt you have read.

The event being so important an one it was made matter for a general day of rejoicing and thanksgiving and orders were given that every house should be illuminated at night, and the "roughs", for they existed then as now, had given notice that they would smash every window in every house that did not display some illuminated device. My Sister, your Aunt Rebecca, and I were taken to spend the day at our Aunt Dickinson's in Summer Hill, where as I told you before I was born. We were much interested in watching the preparations for the illumination—candles in various devices being placed in every front window of the house. After sunset, all these candles were lighted, and we all went through a trap door in the roof on to the flat leads and as the house was on a hill & commanded a very extensive view over the town, we had a grand view of the fireworks which were let off in all directions while guns were fired, and as much noise made as possible.

I was then only a little chap roaming about and watching all that was going on. One day a cart came to the house with coals, and the man that brought them had to carry each sack of coals round to the back of the house through the garden, and then empty the sack through an opening which led down into the cellar under the house. This opening had usually a grated lid or flap, which was set open, while the coals were being put into the cellar.

I had been standing looking at the horse and cart in the road, and then ran down the garden path, turned the corner sharply and forgetting that the grating was not shut, and not being able to stop myself in time, down the hole I went into the cellar.

My head was severely cut, and I was quite stunned. The coal man, who was in the cellar putting the coals tidy, picked me up and carried me up the cellar stairs into the kitchen, and laid me on the kitchen table. It was long before I recovered consciousness—but I distinctly remember opening my eyes, and seeing a lady standing over me bathing my temples while my dear Mother was holding my head—and crying very bitterly, for she thought that I was killed. But God in His great mercy spared my life.

My dear Father at this time was a partner in the firm of Francis, Smith, Dearman and Brunton, carrying on business as Engineers at the Eagle Foundry in Broad St Birmingham, and very often he took me down to the works, where I used to watch with great interest the various operations. I saw them forming moulds for casting in iron and brass all sorts of things, and I was especially interested in a patent grate my father invented, which was at that time being manufactured. It was a self-feeding grate. At the back of the fire was a receptacle for coal which the servant had to fill every morning. At the side of the fire place there was a handle which when turned wound up a weight, connected with the "hopper" or receptacle for coal at the back of the grate.

After the fire was lighted in the morning the servant had nothing more to do in order to keep a good fire all the day—for the hopper kept rising very slowly and as it rose it fed the fire with coals, and at the same time now and then shook the bars at the bottom of the grate to get rid of the ashes. I used to think this a very wonderful thing, and I watched it very often through the day, for one of these grates was put up in our house.

At this time my father had a pupil at the works, a Mr Nicholas Harvey, who was learning the Engineering business—with whom I formed acquaintance in my visits to the foundry. He was a very clever fellow and afterwards, turning his attention to marine Engineering, became the leading man in establishing the Steam boat navigation on the River Rhine which under his fostering care reached very large proportions. He became a man of note.

All this connection with Engineering people gave me a great taste for the Profession and little chap as I was then I determined to be an Engineer. About this time my Father removed from Regent St to a house in Camden St lying at the back of our uncle Dickinson's house on Summer Hill. The garden of our house communicated with the garden of Uncle Dickinson's House, and we Children had the run of both gardens.

[4]

I was a great favorite of my Uncle Dickinson after whom I was named John. He used to take me out for a drive in his gig on many summer mornings —away into the country.

He was very kind and taught me many things amongst others the proper way to drive and manage a horse.

At this period of my life I was learning lessons with my elder Sister Rebecca, and my next brother Robert under a governess and this continued until my Father left Birmingham and removed to London. My Father bought a house in Cannonbury Square Islington, and my brother Robert and I were sent to school at Melbourne in Cambridgeshire kept by a Mr Carver. It was when I was home for our first holidays that an occurrence happened which I shall never forget and of which I feel somewhat proud. The Civil Engineers of that day had determined to form themselves into a Society and to hold meetings periodically for discussion amongst themselves of Engineering subjects.

Thomas Telford was then considered (and deservedly so) the leading man in the Profession and he was elected the first Chairman of the Society, which was called the Institution of Civil Engineers. The enrolled members were at that time few in number, and they met in a room in Buckingham St Adelphi. My father was a member, and one evening took me with him to a meeting of the Institution. Telford was very fond of children, called me to him, and I stood at his knee, while the proceedings were going on. This was in 1823 or 4 when I was between 11 & 12 years of age. From that day I determined to be an Engineer, and during my next holidays, employed myself early in the summer mornings in learning to use the level, starting from our front door step and levelling away along the neighbouring streets and back again to the door step whence I started. I was very proud when after repeated trials I found my levellings correct.

Soon after this I was sent as a student to the Revd Walter Scott of Rothwell in Northamptonshire where a few pupils only were taken who were intended for the learned professions. I was the youngest pupil there, and the idea was to make me a lawyer, a lawyer friend of my Father having proposed to take me into his office when I was old enough. But I cannot say I ever felt the least inclination for that profession.

While I was at Rothwell, the students there were very fond of practical jokes, of which I was often the victim, but the following occurrence put a stop to them altogether. It happened thus.

At our supper hour we all met in the dining room and sat in a semicircle round the fire (there were only eight of us). On a table behind was the bread and cheese and beer, and each one rose from his seat and went to the table to help himself, returning to his seat with his plate in his hand. Amongst our members was a stout young man with whom I had formed a considerable friendship—in fact we were what was called "chums". He was studying specially for the Church.

On the evening in question he had risen to replenish his plate and was backing to his seat when the young man next to him withdrew his chair just as he was sitting down. The consequence was that he went down to the floor backwards very heavily. He lay for a short time insensible—then came on a fearful fit, and it took all present with their united exertions to hold him down—for he was very strong and muscular. We got him by & bye to his bed— but the doctor said the blow on his spine had affected his brain, and he must be watched night and day for he was quite delirious at times.

We students took the watch in turns. I had to go on duty in his room one morning at 5 o'c. The young man I relieved told me he had been sleeping quietly all night, and he appeared to be then asleep. I sat down with my lesson books by the fire. By & bye I heard a rustling, I turned round and saw the patient (his name was Dyer) fumbling in the pockets of his clothes which were on a chair near him.

He looked at me very savagely as I thought, but I asked him what he wanted—his reply was "Brunton if I can find my knife I'll stab you to the heart."

At this moment he had found his knife and jumped out of bed. I thought it was best to make a run for it—so rushed out of the door and down the stairs, he close after me. I fortunately recollected that the lecture room had a bolt on the inside. I rushed in there slammed the door to and shot the bolt in time to stop the pursuit. The noise aroused the household and poor Dyer was secured. It was remarkable that his antipathy was against me only altho' we had been such fast friends.

[7]

The Doctor said this was often the case and I must keep out of his sight—which as may be supposed I was not sorry to do. In a few days his friends arrived and took him home, somewhere in Devonshire, but he never quite recovered—the spine had been permanently damaged,—and in about 3 years he died.

After two years at Rothwell I was considered to be fit to pass the Matriculation Examination for admission to the London University—the first session of which was just opening. I went up and passed—and was entered in the classes of Professor de Morgan for Mathematics, and for French and Latin. I worked hard for two sessions and tried hard for a prize particularly in Mathematics—but there was a young man named McCulloch who distanced us all, carrying every thing before him and I came off with only a *Certificate of Honour*. I then went into my Father's drawing office for a time, and had the advantage of the instructions of my Uncle Robert who was an excellent draftsman.

My Father's office was at the East India Chambers in Leadenhall St and my brother Robert and I had to walk from Cannonbury Square thither every morning. Our route lay along Old Street Road by the side of which in those days, was a sort of grassy common. Along this common was a path which we preferred to the Roadway footpath.

Daily we met a tall gentleman who sauntered along with his mouth wide open. This eccentricity amused us very much. My brother Robert was very fond of jokes. One morning we met him as usual and to my astonishment, for Robert had not told me his intentions, he met the gentleman closely and popped into his open mouth a live blue bottle fly which he had been carrying in his hand. The open mouth closed and crushed the fly. Seeing what was done and anticipating a thrashing we started off as fast as possible followed for a time by the unlucky victim. Though laughing we ran too fast for him and he gave up the pursuit. As you may suppose we took a different route into the city after this exploit, and I think it probable the gentleman kept his mouth closed, at any rate for some time afterwards.

My father at that time was engaged in designing all the machinery for a large lead rolling mill. But what was of more importance to me as affecting my future course, he also had in hand a very important Harbour case, down at Hayle in Cornwall, in which Mr Harvey, the founder and senior partner in the large Foundry and Engine Works at Hayle in Cornwall, was closely concerned.

This Harbour question came on for trial at the Truro assizes. Mr Scarlett, afterwards Sir James Scarlett, was Harvey's leading Counsel—for it was an affair of great magnitude and of vital importance to the interests of Mr Harvey.

The case turned upon Engineering points and my Father, who had grasped the whole question and had made a complete model of the harbour to explain his views and the bearings of the case, gave such good evidence that Harvey gained the case; Mr Scarlett telling him that he owed the victory entirely to my Father's clear evidence, and deductions. Mr Harvey offered to take me into his works as a pupil, without a premium, and to live with him during my pupillage in recognition of my Father's services.

This was at once gladly accepted. Harvey & Co^{ys} works at that time enjoyed the reputation of being the first in the construction of pumping engines and mining machinery of all kinds.

My dear Father accompanied me in the journey down to Hayle; it was a long and weary one in those days. I recollect that we started inside a Coach called the "True Blue", which held six inside! We left London at 1 o'c in the day and did not arrive in Bristol till 6 o'c next morning. I recollect well it was a fine moonlight night and when we stopped for supper at a public house just before we commenced the ascent to Marlboro' Downs, I asked my Father's leave to walk on for the coach being full inside and amongst the passengers a woman with a baby that cried almost continuously I was very tired of the companionship. Well, I walked on and actually passed 6 milestones on the road before the lumbering vehicle overtook me. What should we think of such a mode of travelling nowadays! At the end of the third day we arrived at Hayle and I was most kindly received by Mr Harvey and his sister Miss Harvey and Miss Nanny Harvey, who lived with him and kept his house, for he was an old batchelor. My father committed me to the care of the two old maids who promised to take great care of me for I was only a lad of a little over 16 at the time. Before he left me my dear Father gave me much good advice, assuring me that if I worked hard, I had an opportunity of learning what would be useful to me all thro' life. He gave me his paternal blessing and left me amongst strangers. I felt very lonely, but formed a resolution that with God's help I would not disappoint my dear Father.

Next morning I donned my working suit of fustian and Mr Harvey took me into the works and it was decided that I should commence work in the smith's shop—where my first job was to blow the bellows. The blacksmith I was put under was a kind good fellow and soon put me in the way of striking with the forehammer which was at first very tiring —but practice and determination soon got over that, and I was very shortly classed with about 8 forehammer men or strikers as they were called, who, when the large redhot piece of iron was brought from the fire and laid on the anvil, had to strike it by swinging their hammers round—and it was of course necessary that they should keep very accurate time. I liked this work and soon became proficient at it. Mr Harvey then moved me into the fitting shop—where I had to learn chipping, filing and turning. In those days very much was done by hand which now is done by planing and other machines which have been invented for the purpose of expediting the work as well as ensuring greater accuracy, which is a most important point in the construction of machinery of all kinds. At this time Mr Harvey had a very large order on hand, *viz*. the great Engines for draining the Haarlem lake in Holland. The largest Steam Engines that had ever been made. To my great satisfaction, I was entrusted with the making of a portion of the steam gearing. I had to work from a drawing made on a board, and here, what I had learnt of making drawings and understanding them in my Father's London office was most useful to me. At the next vice of the bench where I worked, wrought a youngster, of about my own age, who was also a pupil—he was Mr Harvey's nephew, a son of the famous Engineer Richard Trevithick, his name was Frank, and we soon became excellent friends—both in the shops and in the evenings after work hours. This was Frank Trevithick who afterwards became Locomotive Superintendent at Crewe—and indeed was the Founder of the enormous establishments now the principal one of the London and North-Western Railway. We had to work the same hours as the men from 6 a.m to 6 p.m—long hours for a youngster, but kind Miss Harvey used to cut me a large slice of bread overnight and gave me permission to go into her fine dairy every morning and place on my bread a thickness of Cornish cream, which was indeed a luxury—and gave me a grand start in the morning. I was moved from place to place in this shop and had opportunities of learning not only chipping & filing—but turning and erecting.

While in these shops I met with a bad accident. I was shifting a very large and heavy Plummer Block on the Bench when its weight overpowered me and it fell coming corner downwards on my right foot—actually punching a piece of the upper leather of my shoe through my foot and breaking a bone of one of my toes. I fainted; I believe the only time in my life, and was carried insensible to my bed.

The old ladies were kindness itself and would not send for the Doctor of the works but undertook to cure me themselves—putting leaves of various kinds upon the wound, which was a large one. For weeks I suffered great pain and the appearance of the wound became ugly.

I begged for the Doctor but the old ladies said they knew of some particular leaves which they would take a long walk and fetch, and they were sure they would cure me. They started one morning on this expedition, when Frank Trevithick came in to see me. I begged him, if he had any regard for me to fetch the Doctor. Fortunately he was seen passing and Frank called him in. After looking at the wound, he said it was just a chance whether I should not lose my foot. He applied caustic and gave me great pain—then strapped my foot round with plaister leaving me wondering what the old ladies would say on their return. Well they came back with the leaves and were astonished to find my foot all bound up—I hardly dared to tell them that I had called in the Doctor, with whom they had had a quarrel, but at last I told them I had done so, and also that he had said I might have to have my foot amputated. This alarmed them—but it was some time before they forgave me. Through mercy the doctor's treatment proved successful and I was shortly able to move about again, to my great delight. To this day however I now and again suffer pain from it—particularly after a long walk.

I now returned vigorously to work to make up for lost time. Shortly after this I went to work in the pattern shop—thence into the Foundry where the castings were made from the patterns—finally I passed through the erecting shop, where the Engines and other Machinery were fitted together. About six months before I had completed my course of instruction the father of Frank Trevithick, the then famous Engineer Richard Trevithick turned up. He had been absent from his family for about 11 years in South America, and had never let his family know where he was—or what he was doing. I saw a good deal of him for he had persuaded Mr Harvey, his Brother in law, that he had invented a great improvement in Steam Engines—by which the Steam having passed through the cylinders was to be pumped back into the Boiler before it condensed. Mr Harvey consented for him to make a trial of his system in the works and I was appointed under his orders to erect the machinery. I soon saw that it was a mistake—but dare not tell Mr R. Trevithick so—for he was a very violent and passionate man. However the Boiler and Engine were completed and tested and then it was shown to be a failure founded on wrong principles. Old Richard Trevithick was very angry about this, and it weighed heavily on his mind so as to derange his judgement. The experiment however was useful to me for it set me thinking and reflecting.

One morning I got a letter from my Father that there was an opening for me in South Wales, and as I had now been at the bench for 2 years he thought I should at once join him in London. This 2 years at Hayle had been a very pleasant time. Mr Harvey had been most kind to me giving me every opportunity of learning the mechanical part of an Engineer's business. I had repeatedly been sent to the mines to look after the machinery and get well acquainted with the mode of working the mines, and dressing the ores.

Mr Harvey not only gave me opportunities of learning matters connected with my profession as an Engineer, but he kept a horse for me and taught me to ride. He encouraged me to learn boating, in the evenings, to practice shooting, and all outdoor manly exercises. While indoors he taught me the art of Carving at table, in which he was a great proficient.

I left Hayle, and my kind friends there with great regret, at the same time I rejoiced at the prospect of seeing my dear Parents and my brothers and sisters again.

II

ON my journey up to London my mind was a
good deal exercised as to the Engineering
job my Father had in view for me. While I
had been at Hayle, George Stephenson had been
moving the minds of the public on the subject of
Railways and I had read from time to time of his
doings,—of the construction of the Line from
Stockton to Darlington, and of a proposal to make a
line between Liverpool & Manchester. I wondered
whether I should ever get any thing to do in this,
which was then quite a novel branch of Engineering.
When I got home, they hardly knew me for I had
grown and had become stout and muscular.

My Father then told me that he had got orders to
construct a line of tramway from the Ynyscedwyn
Iron works—up the Drim Mountain to join an old
tramway on Brecon Forest. The object was to bring
down limestone to the Ynyscedwyn Iron works
where Mr Crane was energetically pressing for-

ward his endeavours to smelt iron with anthracite coal. The construction of the line involved the making a very long and steep incline up the side of the Drim Mountain. My Father could not personally superintend this piece of work, and asked me if I thought I could manage to carry it out as Resident Engineer; I gladly accepted the post. Here was a step at any rate towards becoming a Railway Engineer like George Stephenson, who was then talked about by every one—and whose career I was watching with the greatest interest.

You will recollect that I had practised levelling when I was home from school for the holidays so the use of the level was no quite new thing tho' levelling up the side of a mountain was somewhat different from going along the streets at Islington. Well, I went down to Ynyscedwyn which is nearly at the head of the Swansea valley, far away in the heart of Wales, where very few people indeed spoke a word of English. I felt like a foreigner, and indeed was looked upon as such, by the natives of the district.

I felt very lonely and almost shut out from verbal communication with any one.

However I found out that the principal grocer in the place could speak a little English and could take me into his house as a lodger. I then began to make my survey and take the levels of the line—but I found I could not get on with my staff holders and chainmen, whose reply to any instructions I gave them was "Drin Sassenach"—which means No English so I determined to learn the Welch language. But who was I to find to teach me? I was terribly puzzled. The first Sunday I went to Church, where I had been informed that altho' the Service generally and the Sermon were in Welch, the Litany was always read in English. I was glad to hear this and went fully expecting to understand that portion of the service at any rate. But to my great disgust & disappointment, the Clergyman read it, and the Clerk made the responses, in such a way that I did not recognize the English at all. I bethought myself that I would go and call on the Clergyman, Parson Davies as he was called who was a batchelor and lodged in a small farm house in the valley, and ask him how I could best learn the Welch language. He received me very kindly—but *his* English was very bad.

However a long talk ended in this arrangement that I should come and lodge in the same little farm house as he did. He should teach me Welsh and I was to teach him English. I liked this arrangement because at the grocer's I was pestered with wasps coming after the sugar, and the noise of the men and women coming to make their purchases was most distracting. So I moved bag and baggage, certainly I got away from the wasps—but on the first evening in my little parlour I found I was in for cockroaches innumerable! The Parson came in to spend the evening with me to give me my first Welsh lesson. I got him to give me the Welsh for certain words of command & instructions which I required to manage my men when out surveying. I soon picked these up, not attempting to learn more than colloquial Welsh. I fancy I got more Welch out of the Parson than he got English out of me, for I could soon chatter away and make Taffy understand what I wanted. A few weeks steady work finished my levelling and I sent it up to my Father for his approval, which I shortly received, and I was ordered to engage men and get to work making the cuttings and embankments, building culverts, and one tolerably large Bridge across the Tawe river. I had frequently to go down to Swansea to purchase materials.

Half way to Swansea, lay the little village of Pontardawe. The Clergyman of this Parish was a Mr Price the brother of Dr Price, who was the surgeon settled at Ynyscedwyn, with whom I had made acquaintance. Parson Price lived with his mother and three sisters at the old fashioned Parsonage House. To them I was introduced by the Doctor, and very pleasant recollections I have of their kindness to me, insisting that in my rides into Swansea, I should always make their house a sort of halfway resting house. The distance to Swansea being 15 miles,—a good long ride there and back in the day. Old Mrs Price was a charming old lady and the 3 daughters charming company—so it was a great pleasure to me to drop in there regularly on my journeys. Here I may tell you that the Price family were the descendants of Hugo Price, the Founder of Jesus College Oxford and held certain valuable presentations connected therewith—so they were people of position and highly respected in the neighbourhood.

Amongst the rest of their kindnesses, they gave me a little sharp Scotch Terrier dog, a treasure in his way, as you will soon see.

The works of my line of tramway were getting on well, but I was much troubled with the Welshmen, who if I was not by to watch them were very lazy.

They were a primitive uncivilized race having a great dislike to Englishmen—Saxons as they called them. Petty thefts were common, and they thought an Englishman fair game. I soon found my stock of shirts and handkerchiefs running short, my washer-woman declaring they were stolen off the bushes when she hung them out to dry. I got rather tired of this and warned her that for the future I would make her pay for every article which was missing. The very next Saturday she appeared crying and telling me that one of my silk, canary colored, handkerchiefs had been stolen from her hedge. I told her she must pay for it—it had cost me 6 shillings. This she assented to if I would only stop it by degrees.

The next morning was Sunday and I started to walk to church as usual. The path lay along the river bank. I saw a young man a sawyer whom I regularly employed coming along meeting me. As he neared me I saw he had a silk yellow handkerchief round his neck. I stopped him asking him a question or two about his work—when on looking closer I saw my name clearly at the corner of the handker-chief. I slipped my hand into his neck and got firm hold of him and with a good ash stick I had in my hand I gave him a tremendous thrashing. When I was quite tired I tore the handkerchief off his neck and kicked him over into the river which was not deep—but just enough to give him a good wetting.

I think he deserved this—dont you? Well, the next morning he was at work as if nothing at all had happened. There was no magistrate nearer than 14 miles so I thought perhaps I had given him enough punishment, and that he would not steal my handkerchiefs any more.

About this time I was employing about 500 men and their wages every fortnight amounted to a considerable sum which I was obliged to fetch up all the way from Swansea. I had to bring it up in gold silver and copper for you could not get notes changed up in this wild place, so I had had made a pair of saddle bags to carry the money on horseback. One day I started as usual accompanied by my little dog which as was my custom I left with his old mistress at Pontardawe till my return in the evening. Being late in the autumn daylight had nearly left me, when I arrived at Pontardawe on my return, where I only called to pick up my faithful little Terrier, and proceeded on my journey. The road was dreary and wound through a dense oak wood up a hill.

I was walking my good little horse up this hill my little dog running on ahead of me when suddenly he began to bark furiously at something in the hedge first on one side of the road then on the other. This put me on the alert, I touched my horse with the spurs and came up at a canter. As I approached the point where the wee doggie was still barking two men rushed through the hedge one on each side of the road. Immediately I broke into a galop, steered my horse directly at the left hand man whom he chested when the fellow sprang forward to seize the reins and sent him sprawling on his back. The right hand fellow I struck under the ear with the handle of a heavy hunting whip I had in my hand and sent him also sprawling on the road. I did not stop to see what damage I had done, but galloped on, followed by my little dog, who had been the means of warning me of the danger awaiting me and saving my being robbed of over £400 I had in my saddle bags, perhaps he saved my life. At any rate you may be sure he got a good supper that night, and many an affectionate pat, while I felt most thankful to our Heavenly Father for thus thwarting the designs of those wicked men, and most probably saving my life. After this I got a dog cart and always took a man whom I could trust with me, and a brace of pistols.

Now I will tell you another story. You must know that these poor uneducated Welsh people were very superstitious, they believed in witches and wizards and all such nonsense. There was one old woman living in the parish, who had two sons, one of them by the way was the chap whom I thrashed for stealing my handkerchief. This old woman was a reputed witch and all the people were very much afraid of her, thinking if they quarrelled with her she would do them some harm by bewitching their horses or cows, making the horses lame or stopping the cows from giving any more milk. To such an extent was this dread of the old woman carried that they could refuse her nothing she asked for and so this old woman used to go about from farm to farm and demand a lot of meal from one, a lot of potatoes from another and so on.

She lived in a little out of the way cottage and though she had no land she kept a cow, the fattest in the parish, and she had fowls and ducks, all well fed and comfortable, while she did no work at all. This was very suspicious, was it not?

Well, I wanted to have some hay for my horse so I hired a nice meadow that had a good fence all round it and a good gate, on which I placed a chain and padlock to prevent any animals getting into the meadow while the grass was growing. A week or two passed and I thought I would go and see how the grass was getting on. To my astonishment though I found the gate was fastened as I had left it—the grass had not grown but was evidently eaten off by a cow for I could trace the footmarks. I changed the padlock and determined to watch and try and catch the intruder. Several times I went at nights but could never succeed. It was evident that they kept a look out on my movements. So I determined to try and circumvent them. I gave it out that I was going away for a holiday, and a day or two afterwards, my brother Robert who was with me on a visit, and I, put our portmanteaus into the dog-cart and started off. We only went as far as Pontardawe where we spent the day, and late at night drove back again, much to the astonishment of the farmer's family with whom I lodged, and also of Parson Davies who I am sorry to say was about as superstitious as his flock. It was a dark wet night very favourable for my purpose.

Armed with our whips my brother and I started and I persuaded the parson to accompany us when I told him our errand—he remarking that if he was there he might prevent the witch doing us any injury. I had told him I suspected that her cow was fattening on my grass. On we went and when we arrived at the field, I arranged that the Parson should go down the middle of the field, where there were several tumps of brushwood, my brother down one side of the field and I down the other. We had not proceeded far before the Parson began roaring out "There she is, there's the witch" and commencing running for his life towards the gate. In a very short search my brother and I found the cow quietly reposing under the lea of one of these large bushes. We roused her up and with some difficulty drove her before us to the parish pound. We roused the pound keeper from his bed, and the cow was shut up safely.

My orders were that she was not to be given up without the payment of 30/-.

We trudged home, congratulating each other on the success of our little game, and laughing at Parson Davis who was prophecying that the witch would certainly do us some terrible mischief.

I was roused next morning by a great disturbance downstairs. I listened and soon discovered that it was the old witch demanding the release of her cow. I came down—at first she begged hard that out of compassion I would comply with her request. I talked to her quietly and tried to show her that pilfering my grass in this way was as much stealing as if she had robbed me of my purse, and that I considered I was only doing right in demanding the 30/- which was not half the value of the damage she had done me. Finding I was firm she commenced to threaten all kinds of things. I requested her to leave my room and the house, but she refused to do either, persisting in screaming out threats of every imaginable kind.

At last I took her by the shoulders and put her outside the front door. A little more screaming and she went off. In the afternoon of the same day I was busy making some drawings when in came my waggoner, whom I had ordered to drag up, with his

3 horses, some baulks of timber to the sawpit. He was in a great state of excitement. The witch had bewitched his horses and they would not pull an ounce. "There, I told you so," exclaimed the Parson who had overheard the waggoner's story— "Oh let the cow out of the pound or worse may come of it." I confess I felt very angry—I called my brother to come with me & to bring his whip and away we went to the spot where we found a crowd assembled, the witch amongst them and the 3 horses quietly standing by the baulks of timber.

I ordered the waggoner to hook on the horses to the timber—"I darent, master; no, I darent." I threatened to discharge him if he did not obey my orders, but it was of no avail he literally dare not do it. So my brother and I yoked the horses to the timber and quietly tried to start them. Immediately they came up to their collars, they sprang back and reared up—totally refusing, as the waggoner had said to pull an ounce. This seemed to please the old witch, who kept calling on me to release her cow. I made another trial, coaxing the horses and leading them very quietly up to their work—but with a like refusal. My temper would not stand this, so I called to my Brother to ply his whip vigorously on his side of the team, while I did likewise on the other. Great was the disturbance, but at last—away they went with the baulk of timber at a gallop up to the yard. Convinced that there must have been some reason for this, other than the witch's handwork, I examined the collars of the horses. Why, said I to the waggoner, these are not the collars belonging to these horses—"No master they are not, I took their own collars to be mended this morning, and borrowed these for them to work in." "You fool" said I, "do you not see that these are ponies' collars, far too small for our horses, and when they attempted to pull, the collars choked them?" Such indeed was the case and the cause of all this disturbance.

I warned the witch off the premises—threatening to have her up before the Magistrate if ever she trespassed upon our land again. She found I was not to be frightened, so she and her sons came to me quietly in the evening and gave me a written order to stop the 30/- out of their wages next payday, and I released the cow from the pound.

This belief in the power of witches and wizards shows sad ignorance, but in the next story I am going to tell you how I made use of it in a curious way.

III

THE LITTLE BLACK MARE STOLEN—THE ROAD TO CAR-
MARTHEN—DEFYING THE MAGISTRATE—THE WIZARD
GETS A CONFESSION—THE LITTLE BLACK MARE RETURNS.

ONE Saturday evening I rode home from the
small public house where I had held the *pay*
of the men I had employed on the works—
I rode a favorite little black mare. When I arrived
at the little Farm house where I lodged along with
the parson of the Parish—my stable boy was away
somewhere and I put the mare into her stable myself—hung up the bridle, but took the saddle into
the farm kitchen to be near a fire, for it was damp.

I went to bed as usual very tired after a long
day's work, and next morning lay rather longer in
bed than usual, for it was Sunday morning.

I was awoke by a great deal of chattering downstairs—by and bye the parson knocked at my door.
I opened it and with a face of great consternation he
told me that my good little mare had been stolen
during the night. They had at first fancied she had
somehow strayed away of herself and the boy and

the old farmer had been searching about in the neighbourhood for 2 or 3 hours before telling me.

This was very stupid of them because if they looked they would have seen that the bridle also was gone—and it was not likely that the mare would have put that on to take a ramble by herself. However I was soon dressed and went down to investigate all matters for myself. I went into the stable—saw at once that the bridle was gone, that the mare's head stall was left just as it had been taken off—but under the manger I found another black hair halter, which I knew did not belong to me. I immediately seized it and put it into my pocket thinking it might lead to the discovery of the thief.

It was clear the mare had been stolen. I then recollected that on one of her forefeet she had a bar shoe that is a shoe with a bar across the hind part of it to protect the frog of her foot from the stones on the road; the shape of it being like this. I immediately went out into the road near the house, and the road being soft from the rain which had fallen during the night I soon found the marks of this *bar shoe*. I immediately started off along the road tracing these marks which I followed for about 2 miles, when I suddenly saw that the mare and her rider had turned into a field off the road. At first I was puzzled at this then I recollected that about $\frac{1}{4}$ of a mile further along the road there was a toll bar, and that it was always shut at night so that the thief could not have passed that way without the risk of being recognized, and that knowing this he had gone into this field, and from that into another, which would take him into the road again beyond the toll bar. So I walked on along the road and to my great satisfaction I came again on the prints of the *bar shoe.*

On and on I trudged for some miles until I came to a pathway or bridle track which turned off from the high road right up the mountain and which I knew led on to the Town of Carmarthen, for I had ridden that way myself.

Being very wearied with my long walk & having as yet had no breakfast, I turned back home having got evidence that whoever had stolen the mare had taken the road to Carmarthen.

When I arrived at home I found a considerable group of neighbours collected, all discussing the probabilities of the matter. One old farmer was there who lived not very far off, and he told me that late on the Saturday night before going to bed, he had, according to his usual practice, lighted his lanthorn and gone round his stables and byres to see that every thing was safe. In one of the empty stalls of his stable upon a heap of straw he found a man lying, apparently asleep, he woke him up and demanded what he did there, the man replied that he was tired and had turned in to the stable to sleep for the night. "No, no, my good fellow, this is no place for you; turn out and go to the village", said the farmer. So very reluctantly the fellow got up and went away. I asked the farmer to describe the man, which he did minutely giving me a full description of his face clothes &c so that I immediately recognized from his description that he was one of my workmen to whom I had paid his wages on the Saturday afternoon. I pulled out of my pocket the

[29]

black hair halter I had found in my stable, which the old farmer at once recognized as his—so you see I had a pretty good clue to the thief. But I wanted something more, so next morning, which was Monday I went early to the place where this man ought to have been at work. He was not there. I immediately got the constable of the parish who knew this man by sight and also knew that he came from Carmarthen, and sent him off there to find the fellow and bring him back. In a couple of days the constable returned bringing the man with him handcuffed.

He persisted in denying his guilt, though it was ascertained that he had arrived in Carmarthen at such an hour, that it was impossible he could have walked the distance in the time that had elapsed since he was turned out of the old farmer's stable. Next morning I took him along with the constable and farmer to the nearest magistrate, a distance of 14 miles. The magistrate owed me a grudge for in carrying out my little railway I was obliged to take it thro' a field that belonged to him.

The case was opened before him, but before I could get the evidence laid before him he cut it short and said he could see no reason for my suspecting the man, and ordered the handcuffs to be removed and the man released.

The constable was obliged to obey and the handcuffs were taken off. We were all in a state of utter astonishment, and I was very angry. The constable and I followed the man closely out of the house and off the premises. I immediately called to the constable to seize the man again & replace the handcuffs, which he did most willingly for he as well as I were persuaded we had the guilty horse stealer there.

Into the dog-cart we jumped and I drove off home. On arrival I put the fellow into a small back kitchen telling him that there he should stop and live on bread and water till he told me where my mare was. He protested loudly but I was inexorable.

Guarded by the constable and fed on bread and water my prisoner remained for nearly a fortnight, and I was getting rather alarmed for I had taken the law into my own hands and in fact was not acting legally at all—but what other course had I amongst such a queer uncivilized people. I had daily tried to make my prisoner confess where the mare was, and so had my friend the Parson.

It struck me at last that I might try and take advantage of his Superstitious notions and fears and I told him I should send for the wizard who would tell us all about the robbery. I saw he did not like the idea of this, which made me quite determined to go on with it. You must recollect that he did not know any thing about my having tracked the mare by the bar shoe marks on the road nor had he heard of several other pieces of evidence which I had collected.

So I determined to play the part of the wizard myself. I got a piece of sheep skin and made myself a wig and a long beard. I borrowed some old shawls of my landlady and dressed myself up in a way that perfectly disguised me. The parson was the only one whom I admitted into the secret. The report went through the house that the wizard had arrived and the prisoner was brought out of his cell into my sitting room by the constable.

By and bye, having secured the largest book I could find about the house, which happened to be a Fox's Book of Martyrs, folio size, I placed it under my arm and solemnly entered.

Placing the opened book upon the table, I began to make all sorts of passes and signs with my hands and arms—gazing fixedly on my prisoner who evidently shrunk under my gaze. I then commenced telling him all about where he had been and what he had done on the Saturday in question, going through his visit to the old farmers stable, the abstraction of the black halter, the entry into my stable, the stealing of the mare, the dropping of the halter there—the going along the road till he had come to a certain field, the object of his leaving the road at that point &c &c. As I proceeded I saw the color leaving his cheeks and he began to tremble, then suddenly he dropped down on his knees and told where the mare was. I quietly noted the address down on a piece of paper and then, pulling off my wig, beard, and shawls, I stood before him undisguised.

He started up and at once began to deny that he knew any thing about the mare.

"Well my man," said I, "you will just go back to the cell and your bread and water till I send to Carmarthen and see whether the mare is where you confessed her to be."

[32]

Another constable was despatched next day and in 2 days after he arrived with the mare—having found her at an uncle's of the prisoner where he had said she was—but, poor thing she had been nearly starved and was reduced to skin and bone, nevertheless I was very glad to see her back again for she was a great favorite of mine. She soon got fat again.

IV

SOON after this (about 1830–1) my dear Father
sent for me up to London for a time. He in
conjunction with Messrs George and Robt
Stephenson were employed in trying to get the
London & Birmingham Railway Bill through
Parliament and my Father wished me to be in some
way connected with this important work. Leaving
the works in Wales under my Brother Robert's
charge, I came up to Town and attended all the
sittings in committee of the House on the Bill. It
was very interesting to listen to all the evidence
that was brought forward for and against the making
of this Railway. At any rate the Bill was thrown
out that Session in the house of Lords,—and I returned to Wales and pushed forward the work there.
In the next Session of Parliament the London &
Birmingham Railway Bill was passed, and I received a letter from Robt Stephenson offering me
an appointment as Assistant Engineer upon it at a
Salary of £50 a year more than other Assistant

Engineers because I had been engaged on Engineering works previously. You may imagine how
pleased and proud I was. My Brother Robert took
charge of the completion of the works at Ynyscedwyn and I came up to Town and was placed
under Mr Tho⁵ Longridge Gooch, the District
Engineer of that portion of the line lying between
the Kilsby Tunnel and Birmingham.

He placed under my charge the section from
Kilsby Tunnel to a point about half way between
Brandon village & Coventry. At first however I
had to do levelling & surveying all along the
District, setting out centre lines & other interesting
work. We young Engineers led a very rough life.
We were obliged to work from daylight to dark as
the work was very pressing—and when we started
in the morning we did not know where we were to
get to, that night. The use of the Theodolite in
setting out curves, which has simplified that operation so much was not at that time in practice.
Curves were set out by small offsets at every chain
length. Such offsets being calculated according to
the radius of the curve. When these curves were of
great length and large radius—this became a long
and tedious process. And in those early days, there
was no Ordnance Survey map to help us. However
we got the survey and setting out of the line done,
from Kilsby Tunnel face, to Birmingham, and I was
ordered up to London to take charge of the designing of the necessary Bridge Drawings and other
contract plans for the letting of the works to contractors. The Railway Company took the Eyre
Arms Tavern, at St John's wood as an Engineers
drawing office. The Tavern at that time being unoccupied. The Ball room formed the Drawing

Office. Twenty draughtsmen by day & the same number at night formed the corps I had to superintend, of course under the occasional inspection of my chief District Engineer Mr T. Longridge Gooch.

All the contract drawings had to be ready by a certain day—about a fortnight after the day we commenced the work upon them.

It was a tight pinch, for my draughtsmen then were not much used to this class of work.

But we struggled on—I, very anxious that this, my first important charge should not be behind time, kept at my post night and day with one night only in bed for the fortnight.

This was foolish, as I found out afterwards, but I was full of energy and determination.

One by one my staff dropped off quite overcome with the incessant work I called for, but at last the work was accomplished on the evening before the Contract Plans & Specifications were due in Birmingham.

I had looked them all over—put them all into their special portfolios—and was waiting for the arrival of Gooch with some one, who was to take them in charge and convey them to Birmingham by the night *Mail Coach*. (Recollect there were only 2 Railways in existence then, The Liverpool & Manchester and the Stockton and Darlington.) Every thing being ready I went down to the Entrance and sent for a cab to take me to Edmonton, where my dear Father and Mother were then living.

At that moment I met Mr George Stephenson and Mr Gooch. The latter hailed me: "Halloo Brunton, I can find nobody to take these plans down to Birm^m tonight, so you must take them." I made some slight remonstrance on the head of the work I had gone thro' for a fortnight. But no one else could be found, so the cab which I had hired, with anticipation that it would convey me to a good bed & sleep that night, was loaded with the packages of plans and directed to take me to the *Swan with Two Necks*, Lad Lane, whence the Mail Coach for Birmingham started at half-past eight. I found all full inside and only one of the four outside places left for poor me. I booked for Birm^m, saw my packages safe in the boot of the coach, and got the middle seat of the three behind the coach man. I drew my plaid round my head leaned back against the luggage on the roof and was fast asleep before the coach left the yard. Nor did I awake until $11\frac{1}{2}$ hours afterwards, I was roughly shaken and told I was at the *Hen & Chickens* Hotel Birmingham!

Very stupid I felt, but I deposited the plans, and then, instead of going to my Aunt Dickinsons at Summer Hill, where my dear Sister Maria was then stopping, I took a place in a coach starting for Coventry where I had engaged lodgings, thinking I should go there and sleep quite undisturbed.

Thither I went and immediately retired to bed falling into a sleep, and insensibility which lasted for nearly three weeks. Of the Events of that 3 weeks I knew nothing.

The Doctor searched my pockets and found there a letter of introduction to Mr Witthem then or just previously Mayor of Coventry. To him he sent the letter stating that I was lying dangerously ill. Good & kind Mrs Witthem and her daughter came to enquire after me, and their kindness I shall never forget. They communicated with my sister Maria in Birmingham, who kindly came to nurse me, and through mercy I gradually improved in health, and in about a month I was able to resume my duties on the line under Mr Thomas Longridge Gooch the District Engineer. The portion allotted for my division was that lying between Kilsby Tunnel and nearly to Coventry. On the works of this division I remained till very nearly completed, when through the kindness of Mr George Stephenson & Mr T. L. Gooch I was promoted to the charge of an important district on the Manchester & Leeds Railway (now the Lancashire and Yorkshire).

My district extended from Manchester to the Summit Tunnel near Todmorden.

I was succeeded on my London & Birmingham Division by Mr Meek.

I cannot resist telling you of one amusing occurrence which happened to me early in my engagement on the Manchester and Leeds line.

Mr George Stephenson came down and as was his custom took one of the Engineers with him to act as his Secretary during a journey through the District traversed by the Railway.

We were at Wakefield in Yorkshire one day, when Mr Stephenson called me and said, "Brunton order a chaise quick, we must be in Manchester in time for me to catch the train to Liverpool this evening."

I looked at my watch and saw that to do this, there was not a minute to spare; I had the chaise at the door sharp and Mr Stephenson & I jumped in, with injunctions to the post boy to drive fast. On we went and when approaching the toll bar at Littleborough, I sat with a shilling in my hand to pay the toll without losing time. The chaise pulled up and from the toll house came out a man with leather apron on and a last in his hand. Mr S. seeing him called out "Halloo, ye are a shoemaker are ye." Ay said the man. Quoth Mr S. "do ye ken how to mak cobbler's wax?" No Sir, says the man I generally buys it. "What! you a shoemaker and dinna ken hoo to mak cobler's wax! Open the door. Open the door." But, Mr Stephenson said I we have no time to spare we shall miss the Train. Man! said he, here's a shoemaker doesna ken hoo to mak Cobbler's wax.

With that he entered the toll house, and with a pot over the fire he showed the wondering cobbler how to make cobbler's wax.

Of course we missed the train, and all the way from Littleboro' to Manchester I was treated to a most interesting lecture, upon the advantage to every man to be self reliant and in business of every kind to make himself master of every step or stage in such business.

About this time I went to Glasgow on a visit to my future Father in law. On my return I was the only passenger in the stage coach or rather the *mail* coach. I had the seat by the driver, when we were approaching the boundary line between England & Scotland near Gretna Green we noticed that the turnpike gates were closed and on the Scotch

[39]

side of them there stood a chaise and four horses—
the latter in a fearful sweat. The guard blew his
horn vigorously but no one came to open the gates
so we were obliged to stop. Immediately out rushed
the toll bar keeper eagerly urging the guard and
myself to come into his house and witness a marriage
between a lady & gentleman who were inside waiting
for witnesses. The guard & I got down and went into
the house. There were the couple—the lady weeping
bitterly, the gentleman doing his best to comfort her.

The toll keeper came forward and taking hold of
a hand of each placed them together while reciting
some form of words. He then pronounced them
man and wife and called on the guard and myself
to witness the ceremony by signing a paper which
he put before us. We signed it. He handed us a
tumbler of whiskey and water each, the newly
married couple got into the chaise at the door and
away they went at a galop towards Glasgow.

We also mounted the mail coach, the gates were
opened and we went off, also at a quick speed towards Carlisle.

We had not gone a mile when we saw a chaise &
four coming at a galop an old gentlemans head and
shoulders out of the window. As he came near we
shouted to him "Too late Sir, too late." This
caused the head & shoulders to retire into the chaise.
On we went laughing heartily and congratulating
ourselves that we had witnessed a "Gretna Green
marriage".

But I have forgotten to mention a circumstance
which occurred to me while carrying on the works

[40]

on the London & Birmingham Line which is of interest in many ways.

While making the cutting for the Railway near Coventry, in the new Red sandstone formation, one day when I was standing at the easterly end of the cutting, some loaded wagons were running down towards the embankment as they passed one piece of stone fell from a wagon, in falling it broke across the middle and disclosed a hole in the heart of the stone out of which fell a live toad. I immediately picked it up, as well as the two broken pieces of rock.

I placed the toad on the stone and the poor animal injured about the head in the fall crawled back to the hole it had inhabited for so many hundreds of years.

I carefully carried it up to our office in Hertford St. Great was the sensation caused in the city of Coventry when the news of a live toad being found embedded in the sandstone rock was circulated.

Crowds came to see it, and I was principal exhibitor. I clayed him up in his den every night. When first discovered he was of a bright yellow color, but he gradually became brown, and evidently was suffering from the damage he had received, one eye being crushed.

On the tenth day he died and I put him into a bottle of spirit.

The Railway Directors heard of this "find" and demanded that I should give it up as they had passed a resolution presenting the curiosity to the Birmingham Museum.

A full statement of all the particulars of its being found was drawn up & signed and forwarded to the Museum where I believe it now is. Since that time other instances have been discovered.

Now for another curious "find". On the line of the London & Birmingham Railway I had to build a viaduct over the River Avon between Wolston & Brandon Villages.

On examination as to the foundations to be expected I discovered that below the bed of the river there were 25 feet in depth of peat lying on a bed of firm gravel. This I found out by pushing down a long bar of iron.

To reach the gravel it therefore became necessary at each of the abutments and piers of the viaduct to construct what are called coffer dams, formed of planks driven down through the peat and into the gravel to enable us to build up the foundations.

When the coffer dam was complete, we of course had to excavate the black peat.

On arriving within about 5 feet of the gravel we found complete trees lying of course on their sides with all their branches crushed down quite flat; but you may imagine our surprise to find quantities of hazel nuts in the peat amongst the branches. Of course they were very black and soft. I took out a large quantity of them hoping to dry and keep them as a curiosity—but as they became dry they crumbled to dust. We went on sinking in the same character of black stuff formed of coarse peat till the gravel bottom was reached, but here our surprise was doubled for, lying on the surface of the gravel we

[42]

found skulls of the short horned breed of oxen, quite complete teeth, horns and all, with a great number of bones not only of oxen but of sheep, hares & foxes and, most wonderful of all, the leg bone of an elephant! These discoveries were made in each of the coffer dams. Most carefully I took them to my lodgings and cleaned them, eventually packing them in three casks. I confess I did not say much about this discovery at the time as I was afraid that the Company might do as they did about the live toad in the rock and take them from me. Perhaps I was wrong in this, and as it turned out it was unfortunate. I always carried these 3 casks about with me for several years afterwards as part of my baggage till I was living near Workington in Cumberland where I made the acquaintance of Doctor Dickinson, a medical man there, who I found in conversation to be a great naturalist.

One of his theories being the antiquity of the short horned breed of cattle. I mentioned my discoveries at the River Avon, opened my casks and rejoiced his eyes, with a view of a substantial confirmation of his pet theory.

He had a considerable collection of specimens in Natural History, so when I left Workington and in consideration of much kind attention he had shown me, I presented him with the contents of the 3 casks to add to his museum.

Some years afterwards, when in Turkey, I heard of Dr Dickinson's death. Again after several years I wrote to make enquiries as to the existence of his museum, and heard from his daughter, that she unfortunately could give me no information about it, she believed it was dispersed. This I greatly regret.

V

MARRIAGE—MISCELLANEOUS EMPLOYMENT—ENGINEER-
ING ADVISOR AT PLYMOUTH—MEETING WITH BRUNEL—
THE CRIMEAN WAR—SUMMONED TO THE WAR OFFICE—
RED TAPE—HER MAJESTY'S COMMISSION—A HURRIED
JOURNEY—THE SMYRNA HOSPITAL—A GOOD BONFIRE—
CONSTANTINOPLE—THE SEARCH FOR A HOSPITAL SITE—
THE DESPATCH BOX LOST—MEETING WITH MISS NIGHTIN-
GALE—SITE FOUND AT CHANAK—EMPLOYING 3000 MEN—
THE DESPATCH BOX FOUND.

Now I will go back to the time when I was
district Engineer on the Manchester and
Leeds Railway which passed with only one
very important event to record, which was that I met
your dear departed Grandmama at Mr Cleggs in
January 1839 and we were married on the 29th of
April following. This was the commencement of a
happy 40 years of married life, with which a Kind
Providence blessed me and which I look back upon
with great thankfulness. Your dear "Ama", as you
loved to call her, was the companion of all my future
wanderings, my solace in troubles and illnesses and
my wise advisor in many difficulties.

Soon after our marriage the Manchester and
Leeds line was opened, and Mr George Stephenson
offered me the Chief Engineership of the Maryport
and Carlisle Railway, which was then just commenced. We went down there and I entered on my
duties, which were not of long continuance, as there
are no heavy works on the line.

I was then appointed Manager of some Iron works at Workington called Seaton Iron works. I was not long there as one of the Partners and I could not agree as to the economical mode of carrying on the works and I left.

I then took a lease of a piece of land on which there was a fine vein of firebrick clay, which I developed, starting firebrick making, which turned out of such excellent quality that I was offered a price for the whole going concern which I accepted.

While engaged in this adventure I was appointed superintendent of the building of a new College at St Bees, which I visited periodically until its completion. The Contractor was Mr Thomas Nelson of Carlisle an excellent man with whom I formed a friendship I shall always look back upon with much pleasure.

I then went down to my father-in-law's print work at Ruthvenfield to put his machinery in order. While there my brother-in-law's works at Kincaidfield were burnt down and I went there to superintend their re-erection and to arrange new machinery.

Meanwhile your dear Father was born on the 26th January 1840, and was the delight of our eyes.

Passing over some years of miscellaneous employment, I was engaged by Messrs Hutchinson and Ritson, large contractors under Mr Brunel as their Engineering advisor on their several Contracts which were heavy and numerous. They had in hand the Great Western Mill Bay Docks at Plymouth— the Lee Moor Railway—The Yeovil branch and the

Wilts, Somerset & Weymouth Railway. You may imagine that we had a great deal of moving about.

We lived at Plymouth for a time on Mutley plain —when there your dear Father was at school at Ivy Bridge. After sundry moves amongst others to Bridgewater, we resided at Dorchester where the heavy works of the Wilts Somerset and Weymouth were in progress.

Naturally the construction of these works brought me frequently into communication with Mr Brunel.

This was at the commencement of the Crimean War, and in the depth of a severe winter. The daily Papers teemed with accounts of the sufferings of our Soldiers from the cold and the deficiency of hospital accommodation for the sick and wounded. All England was stirred, and it was determined to start Civil Hospitals, that is, Hospitals supplied with Physicians and Surgeons from the civil not military ranks—but paid by Government. Prompt action was taken and Volunteers of the Medical profession proffered their services. Though much engaged with my Railway duties, I used in the evenings to read all the Newspaper accounts to your dear "Ama" and my dear Cousin Kate Brunton who was then stopping with us and we were all deeply interested. Your dear Father was then at the Grammar school in Dorchester.

One day I recd a telegram from Mr Brunel requesting me to come to Town by that night's mail and be at his office by 6 o'c next morning! Great was our wonder what this was about, and various the guesses made while discussing this very extra_ ordinary summons. I took my seat in that night's mail and arrived in Town on a dark cold wintry morning.

At 6 o'c I presented myself at 19 Duke St Westminster. A footman in livery opened the door, and told me in reply to my enquiry that Mr Brunel was in his office room expecting me. I was ushered into the room blazing with light, and saw Mr Brunel sitting writing at his desk. He never raised his eyes from the paper at my entrance, I knew his peculiarities, so walked up to his desk and said shortly "Mr Brunel I recd your telegram and here I am." "Ah" was his reply "here's a letter to Mr Hawes at the War office in Pall Mall, be there with it at 10 o'c." He resumed his writing and without a word further I left his office, and went and got my breakfast more puzzled than ever, as to the meaning and upshot of all this. At 10 o'c, you may be sure I was at the War office, was at once shown in to Mr Hawes' room who at once plunged into the matter after perusal of Mr Brunel's letter. He told me that the Government wanted an Engineer to go out to take charge of the Sanitary & other requirements of the temporary Hospitals being established at Smyrna and Abydos and to superintend the erection of a large Hospital of 3000 beds, at some place as near the front as possible; the Engineer would have to select the site and superintend the works. All this nearly took my breath away. Mr Brunel had strongly recommended me to Government as the Engineer for this important duty, Mr Hawes asked me whether I would accept it. After a moment's reflection upon the grave responsibilities of such an appointment I boldly said "yes if he & I could agree upon certain important

[47]

preliminaries ". To the discussion of these we turned immediately.

Mr Hawes asked what pay I required I asked a modest sum, to which he immediately assented, I saw at once I had asked less than he had been prepared to give—but it was done I could not draw back. After detailing all my duties which were numerous, he told me that for all stores and supplies of materials or men I should have to apply to the Royal Engineer in charge of the District who would communicate with the War Office. On this important point I joined issue—I saw that if my hands & feet were thus to be bound with *red-tape* (as we call it) the important work would never be completed either to my credit or to the attainment of the end in view.

This I stated plainly and firmly—I said I must be perfectly free to act promptly on all occasions that might arise and to be in a position to employ what men I required & purchase such materials as I deemed necessary. We argued this point for at least an hour, I stuck to my colours, convinced that I was right.

He got rather angry. "What were your expences coming up here" he asked—I named the sum. He immediately wrote out a cheque—"There" said he "is a cheque for your expences & 10 guineas for your time & trouble—you will get the cash for the cheque down stairs good morning."

I took the cheque, got it cashed below and immediately took a cab to Duke Street to see Mr Brunel, thank him for his good intentions in my behalf and explain where Mr Hawes and I had differed. This I did and in silence Mr B. listened to my full statement of the case. When I ceased all I got was "Brunton, you are a fool! I thought to do you a good turn." With thanks and a bow I left his office, took my seat in that night's mail and returned to the anxious ones I had left at Dorchester.

Of course I had to go through the whole of the story again, and long was the discussion we had as to my being too exacting or not. I had made the acquaintance of a military man quartered at Dorchester. I went to him & told him the whole story again. His knowledge of the service enabled him to assure me I was perfectly right in what I had demanded and he told me I had not asked enough on several important points. However I said it is all too late now. I went home and had a good sleep after my two nights travelling. In the course of the day, I was astonished to receive a summons from the war office to be there at 10 o/c next morning.

Another nights travelling, and I presented myself again before Mr Hawes, feeling more firmly seated in my saddle than on the former occasion.

Mr Hawes commenced with another attempt to break me down in my demands for *carte blanche*.

I told him that not only did I stand by all my previous demands as to the powers to be placed in my hands, but I had others.

He was angry—tossed me a sheet of paper and told me to write out what I meant by *carte blanche*. This I did, demanding not only what I had done before but in addition that the Commissariat should have orders to pay all accounts, certified by me, that I should receive Her Majesty's commission as a Field Officer (Major) in the Service, and be entitled to draw all the allowances, rations, &c to which that rank in the service entitled me. This was important, as my military friend at Dorchester had told me, for it gave me in addition to my pay, the keep of two horses, double rations for myself and two servants.

This document opened the discussion again more severely than ever, but I would not yield one point. At last Mr Hawes said "You are very hard to deal with, but I suppose you must have it." He then signed my sheet of terms, ordered a copy to be made of it, and handed me the original. "Now", said he, "you must be on duty this day week, I cannot give you longer." This staggered me, but I agreed to it, trusting that I could make arrangements with my Employers, Hutchinson and Ritson.

On leaving and when he handed me my signed terms of Engagement Mr Hawes said, "There Mr Brunton, you have now in your hands greater powers than any other officer in Her Majesty's service. I feel sure you will not abuse them." He sent me down to be introduced to Mr Milton of the Commissariat Department, about whom more hereafter. Rather proud of my success in this interview, I went to Mr Brunel's office. He was in, I walked up to him, and said "Be good enough to read that, Mr Brunel." After reading it he said "Well Brunton, I did not think you could have got it." My reply was "Then you do not think me such a *fool* as at our last interview." Immediately his manner to me changed, he became quite confidential, and told me all the advice he had given to Government as to the erection, character, &c of the New Hospital.

When I mentioned the difficulties which I feared with Messrs Hutchinson & Ritson,—"I will soon settle *that*", said he; and he at once wrote a letter to them that *they must* allow me to leave *at once*. I mentioned that I had a pupil, Mr Henry Waring, who had still some year and a half to serve with me. "Send him into my office" said he "I will take him without any premium." Of course I expressed my obligations to him for all this kindness, and started back to my dear ones at Dorchester, electrifying them with all the incidents connected with my successful visit to Town. No time was now to be lost.

Hutchinson and Ritson at once agreed to Mr Brunel's request. Balanced up my account for services with them, and with a handsome letter sent me £100 extra. Henry Waring was much pleased with the prospect opening out before him, and as you may suppose, so was I. The only bitter portion was the prospect of separation for an indefinite time from my family. I believed I was in the path of duty and prayed for help and guidance therein.

Within the week I was again at the War office. Information had arrived that the Hospitals at Balaclava were full, that a ship load of sick and wounded had been sent off to an *empty* Turkish Barrack at Smyrna where the poor fellows were lying on the floors, no beds, no clothes but a blanket apiece.

My orders from the War office were—Buy and send out *every thing necessary* to furnish this Smyrna

Hospital, capable of containing 1000 sick. Dr Meyers had been appointed as Principal Medical officer on this the first of the Civil Hospitals. I immediately went and saw him. He had sent out a number of medical men and orderlies. Miss Stanley had organized and started with a party of lady nurses—he told me, and now I must despatch every thing else. What this *every thing else* included we discussed and settled. I at once went to work and spent a large sum (nearly £25,000) in the course of a week. Beds, bedding, stoves, coal, cooking apparatus &c &c &c. I engaged steamers, and reported myself ready to start overland. I had received a special commission in the Army Works Corps—30 of these men (carpenters, joiners, fitters, &c.) were ordered to go out with me overland, through France to Marseilles where a steamer was to be in waiting for us. Your dear "Ama" and your Father were up in London to see me off—we had lodgings in Craven St Strand. I had arranged for my Army Works Corps fellows to meet me at London Bridge Railway Station to start by a Train for Dover at 10 o'c on Sunday morning and had taken all tickets &c. Weary with all my work and anxieties, we retired to rest on Saturday night packed and all ready for the morning's start.

I woke pretty early in the morning and looked out, what was my consternation at perceiving the ground covered thickly with snow, and still snowing. I sent the servant out to get a cab. None to be got, they would not turn out in 4 inches of snow and on Sunday morning too! I was in despair. I rushed over to the Golden Cross Hotel, summoned the "Boots" whom I knew and told him to try what he could do—I offered £1 for a cab. With my watch in my hand counting the minutes, I waited his return. "No use Sir" said he, "they will not turn out. Where's your luggage?—we will run down to Hungerford Stairs and try to catch a boat." No sooner said than done! My portmanteau and one bag in his hands the rest in mine, hurried farewell kisses—and we race all the way to the stairs, just in time to catch a miserable looking passengerless steam boat bound for London Bridge.

Still looking at my watch and knowing that these boats called first at the Middlesex side before crossing to the Surrey side & that following such a course I should certainly miss my train. I told my tale to the Skipper on the Bridge and begged him to take the Surrey side first. He said he could not do it. I rushed aft to the man at the wheel, told my tale again, slipped 5s. into his hand and begged him to make a mistake for once and steer to the Surrey side first. I saw the skipper eyeing us over his shoulder, with a smile on his face, from which I augured success. And sure enough to the Surrey side we went. I jumped ashore, caught a porter, ran up to the Railway Station, arriving just as they were closing the gates to the Train, breathless but thanking God for having prospered me on this first pinch. My fellows received me heartily and we were off.

On, on, through Calais & Paris &c to Marseilles where I found the Steamer awaiting us could not accommodate more than my fellows—whom I put on board, and with Dr Meyers secretary, Mr Chas Goolden, I took berths in a Messagerie Impérial Steamer just starting for Smyrna. We had a good passage and arrived before the special steamer.

On landing at Smyrna I went at once to the Hospital to report myself to the officer in Military charge who was Colonel Storks (now Sir Henry Storks)—who had been informed of my coming. With tears running down his cheeks he embraced me kissing me on both cheeks. I shall never forget that embrace and what it implied. Here was relief come to over a thousand of his poor fellows lying sick and wounded without beds, fire, or any comforts or alleviation of their misery. In a few hours the steamer from Marseilles arrived bringing Dr Meyers and my detachment of Army Works Corps fellows. With Dr Meyers and Colonel Storks I went through the whole of the Hospital, where we saw what I shall never forget. The poor fellows, sick and wounded, lying on the bare boards of the floors and corridors with nothing but a dirty blanket apiece to protect them from the cold, which was then severe.

After a consultation with Dr Meyers it was decided that I should first take the dimensions of the several wards to settle the number of patients to be accommodated in each. This I did and we found that allowing the proper number of cubic feet of space for each patient, the barrack was not nearly sufficient for all. Further hospital room must be found, of which I went in search through the place and discovered a large old abandoned Lazarette, of which we took possession and I set my men to work to clean and whitewash it.

In the meantime my 4 steamers had arrived with all the stores I had purchased in London—beds, bedding, stoves, coal &c &c—which were soon unloaded and distributed through the wards. The thankfulness expressed on the faces of the poor sufferers, was only equalled by that which not only I, but the medical officers, nurses, orderlies &c experienced on finding such a happy change in their condition. All around the wards or barrack rooms there were bunks or boxes with locked lids, in which the Turkish soldiers, used to keep their several kits. They were the nests of millions of bugs, who on the wards being warmed by the stoves, came out amongst the patients and caused great discomfort. My orders were, "out with these bunks". My men soon had them out and we piled them up in the centre of the Barrack square—making a most respectable bon-fire, where millions of bugs perished.

The drains and sanitary arrangements I found in a fearful state, and much had to be done to put them into any thing like a proper condition. While thus occupied I received orders to go up to Constantinople to meet Dr Parkes who was appointed P.M.O. to the Civil Hospital of 3000 beds which I was to erect on some site to be selected by me for it. The nearer to Balaclava or "the front" the better. Leaving full instructions as to carrying out the improvements at Smyrna I started for Constantinople with all my luggage amongst it my despatch box containing amongst other documents of importance some trust deeds of Mrs Barbers estate which had been sent to me for signature, while I was at Smyrna.

On arriving at Constantinople I found Masiree's Hotel quite full, and could only find accommodation at a small Hotel kept by a Maltese.

There I took up my quarters, and having met and consulted with Dr Parkes, it was decided that I should start with a small party consisting of a Dragoman and guides to search for a site for the Hospital on the borders of the Black Sea, towards Trebizond. The prospects of comfort or even safety on this expedition were not encouraging, but it appeared to be the line of my duty. Before starting I summoned the Landlord of my Hotel, showed him the luggage I was leaving in his charge, and gave him a copy of a list I had made out. Amongst this luggage was a deal box in which I placed a new suite of clothes and my despatch box—which was in a leather case having on it a brass plate with my name on it. The lid of the deal box was screwed down by myself—indeed no one was by while I packed up every thing—for I only took with me a small leather bag with changes of linen.

I handed to my landlord 40 sovereigns & took his receipt for the whole. He promising to put my luggage into his locked up box room.

We were to travel on mules—there being no roads and no other means of conveyance.

We started and I cannot describe the horrors of this desolate & weary journey thro' nearly uninhabited districts along the coast.

Wherever there was any appearance of a probably favorable site for the Hospital, of course I had to examine it, this was interesting enough, it was the fearfully filthy state of the huts, I cannot call them houses, where we had to put up for shelter at night—no beds but every place swarming with bugs and fleas.

So very little rest was to be got and the food was

execrable. After examining various localities, I was convinced that the absence of all good water, and the evidently malarious influences of the coast, traceable in the miserably unhealthy appearance and condition of the few wretched inhabitants we encountered rendered it quite unsuited for my purpose and I turned my steps back again, determining to examine the borders of the Bosphorus.

While we were riding along the precipitous banks of the Bosphorus, my party got slightly ahead of me. I came to a rocky gully across which the scarcely traceable track led; at the bottom of this gulley was a small stream trickling over the rock. My mule who though rather lazy had behaved pretty well throughout the journey, stuck out his forefeet and totally refused to cross the stream. I tried coaxing but failed, I then applied my spurs, double barrelled, the brute gathered himself together and made a jump, at least four feet from the ground over the stream—in doing this he burst the girths, and saddle and I were pitched on to the rocks. I was stunned and lay there till my people came back to see what had become of me, my saddleless mule having gone forward and joined their cavalcade.

Fortunately, within a short distance was a small hamlet and a small Turkish hospital.

To this they carried me. Turkish surgeons being educated in Paris all speak French so I was able to explain matters. They treated me with the greatest kindness—bound up my cut arm, gave us some refreshments which we sorely needed and we started for Constantinople, not many miles away. On entering the city I met the British Consul—"Why" said he "you look seedy" so I told him the history of my journeyings. He kindly ordered his Dragoman to take me across to Stamboul to the Turkish baths there—and he told me to give myself up entirely to the people there. He had told them to give me a good bath,—and so they did taking $3\frac{1}{2}$ hours about it, but with astonishing effects. I came out as fresh and vigorous as if I had not been living a life of misery for some time before besides meeting with that unlucky accident.

I assure you I felt most thankful. After a nights rest I summoned the Landlord of the Hotel and demanded my money & baggage. He brought me my money and I went with him to the boxroom. Immediately I saw that the wooden box formerly mentioned had been tampered with, I looked in—it was empty; my new suit of clothes and above all my despatch box were gone. The landlord was aghast and I indignant and threatening serious consequences to him. I went at once to the British Consul and told him of the circumstances begging his help to get me back my despatch box at least. He put the whole matter in the hands of the police, such as they were, and informed me, much to my distress, that probably I should never recover my lost property. After reporting the unsuccessful result of my explorations on the borders of the Black sea to Dr Parkes and the British Ambassador, I was instructed to continue my search for a site westward, down the Sea of Marmora—and a small steamer was placed at my disposal.

Before starting I crossed over to Scutari and had an interview with Miss Nightingale which was very interesting to me. I told her about the Smyrna

Hospital and what Miss Stanley and her lady nurses were doing. She condemned the system of lady nurses, what she said she wanted was a corps of trained hospital nurses. From what I had seen then and afterwards, I quite agreed with her. She is a wonderful business-like woman.

I then called again on the Consul begging him to do all in his power for the recovery of my lost despatch box. This he kindly promised but gave me no hope.

I then sailed for Prinkipo—an island in the sea of Marmora. I found there an excellent site as far as healthiness and position were concerned but there was a grave deficiency of water at all times and during the summer water had to be brought in barges from the main land. I searched all along the coasts of the Sea of Marmora—far more comfortably than I did the coast of the Black Sea, and at last reached the Dardanelles where a few miles west of the principal Town of the Dardanelles called Chanak Kalehsi I found a splendid site combining all my requirements as to natural formation, supply of water and freedom from malaria. I ascended the rather precipitous hills lying immediately to the south and found fine springs of water. The village of Renkioi lay on the top of the hills about 2 miles to the Southwest. I immediately drew up my report & sent it to Constantinople receiving almost immediately an order to fix upon the site and to commence laying out the Hospital. Ships and steamers loaded with material from England were already in the Dardanelles waiting my orders. I commenced work at once. 150 army works corps men were placed at my disposal and under my military command. Greeks were engaged and very soon we made a goodly show of work. A long row of officers quarters was erected early in the work and none too soon, for about 25 medical men had arrived, many of them with their wives and children, and of course were clamorous for dwellings.

Nurses and orderlies arrived, all of whom had to be put up somehow. For a time tents were used. I had been living in a tent until at last I got one of the Officers quarters. I had about 3000 men at work, mostly Greeks. Turks will only do certain kinds of work, they will sail boats for landing or conveying stores, and they will lay water pipes and build reservoirs for storing it, but they wont do Carpenters work.

As you may suppose we became quite a colony. We had no Chaplain so I ran up one of the timber wards, called it the Church Ward, paraded my Army Works Corps fellows every Sunday morning marched them to Church, & read the Service and one of Kingsleys Sermons. These services were soon attended by all the Europeans in the station and I believe were prized. This went on for eight months, when I was summoned up to Constantinople on some important business again. I went up in H.M.S. *Oberon* (Captain Freeland). On my arrival in the Golden Horn I immediately landed and rushed up to the British Consulate to ask if any thing had been heard of my despatch box. "No nothing", said the Consul "I told you to give it up long ago." Next day it was very hot and Captain Freeland & I were walking along in Pera when it became suddenly overcast and much to our astonishment it began to pour with rain—a circumstance quite unusual at that time of year.

"This won't do; we must shelter somewhere", said Captn F. "come along to the office of our coal merchant. I do not know him but my uniform will pass us in."

We rushed down a very narrow street leading to Galata and into the dark office room of the coal merchant. A clerk was there but his master was out. We apologised for the intrusion and were asked to take seats which we gladly did.

The room or outer office was large, dark, and very lofty—round the walls were shelves containing miscellaneous packages. As we sat my eyes became accustomed to the darkness and I kept looking round the shelves. On a top shelf, up in a corner I saw to my astonishment something very like my despatch box. I confess I felt some hesitation about mentioning the matter to the clerk in charge—but at last I said: "Some nine months ago I lost a despatch box, and I see up in the corner there something very like it." "Oh" said he "if that is yours I could tell you about it." He fetched a ladder and brought down the box—thickly covered with dust wiped it & I looked at the brass name plate. "Captain Freeland said I, is that my name?" "Of course it is" said he, "what's the meaning of this?" I took out my bunch of keys, selected the key I knew ought to open it and astonished the clerk and Captain by doing so. What was my astonishment, delight and thankfulness to find every thing intact.

I related all the circumstances of its loss, and then the Clerk told me that about nine months before— one evening when his master had left & he was in the inner office sorting the papers, he heard the outer door opened, some one rush in bang something down on the counter, and immediately rush out again, so quickly, that he could not catch sight of him. On the counter was this despatch box. Next morning he told his master the circumstance. They read the name on the plate, and his master concluded that the owner had left it in passing, and would likely call for it next day. It was placed on a lower shelf, but during the months which elapsed it had gradually been removed higher and higher till it had reached the topmost corner where I had recognized it. I walked off with my box triumphantly—wondering at the strange coincidences —the unusual shower, the accidental companionship of a man who knew of a place of shelter—and that place the very spot where my box was lying.

You, my dear Jack, have that despatch box now— take care of it, and be sure that if you were to lose it, the probabilities are you would not find it again in the marvelous way I have told you about.

VI

WHILE on this visit to Constantinople I was sent for to the Scutari Hospital to advise with Colonel Storks, who had been transferred from Smyrna to the command at Scutari, about some improvements that were required. It ended in Scutari Hospital being put under my charge.

I returned to Renkioi, during my absence good work had been done.

The Government had raised a corps of Bashi-Basouks recruited from all quarters. The corps was encamped about 9 miles from Renkioi.

Three of the cavalry troops consisted of Albanians recruited from the Banditti of that province.

One evening at dusk I was sitting at my tent door smoking a chibouk (Turkish pipe) when I saw approaching my camp along the Bridle path leading from Chanak Kalehsi a column of cavalry. As the path passed in front of my tent I saw that every man was loaded with plunder—sheep, fowls, geese, sacks of grain &c and what astonished me most was that they carried English colours. Not a word was spoken till the rearguard was passing, when they shouted in their broken language "Inglese no bono"— meaning "the English were not good".

I immediately suspected danger, wrote a note to the Consul at Chanak Kalehsi—informing him what I had seen, and despatched it by mounted messenger. Waiting and watching from my hut on a piece of rising ground, I heard, about 11 o/c at night, the beat of the paddles of a steamer. I soon saw her lights and that she was coming into our western bay pier. I rushed down and almost immediately 3 or 4 ships longboats came to the pier loaded with Turkish soldiers.

The Consul's brother was in command—I told him what I had seen and he informed me that these 3 troops of Bashi-Basouks had mutinied and had been plundering the country they had passed through murdering several of the farmers who had resisted them.

They had announced their determination to plunder his brother the Consul's country house in the Village of Renkioi.

The Consuls mother and 2 sisters were then residing there and he and the Turkish troops were on their way—no hopes to arrive in time for their protection. I pointed out the route these Albanian rascals had taken and suggested his taking a shorter but steeper path up the mountain. He recommended me to send all the ladies and children in my camp on board the steamer in which he had come and which was ordered to remain in the offing and then said he "Muster all the men and arms you have and defend yourselves for these rascals will be sure to attack and if possible plunder your camp and stores." This was far from agreable news and advice, I immediately went round rousing every body and ordered all the ladies & children to go on board the Steamer—great was the consternation, the weeping and wailing, mixed with some attempts at opposition to my orders. I was peremptory and we packed them all off.

Then the order was "Muster all the arms in the camp"—alas they were but few, principally fowling pieces and no bullets.

Fortunately amongst the orderlies were some old seasoned soldiers. I set them to cast bullets—and in the meantime despatched a note to the Captain of an East Indiaman that was lying in the Straits— telling him the story and begging him to land as many of his crew as he could spare and what muskets he might have in his armoury.

The good fellow as soon as he got my note mustered a lot of his men and came ashore with them bringing 2 9 lb canonades and 27 stand of musket with a lot of ammunition.

This reinforcement eased my mind a good deal. By this time it was morning and I was obliged to turn military Engineer and posted the guns in the situation I thought best for the protection of my camp, and got all the men into something like order. I posted sentries and with rolls of roofing felt formed a regular fortification. Of course all work at the hospital buildings was at a stand.

I wrote asking for a military guard of either English or Turkish troops. In the course of a few days 3 companies of Turkish troops arrived. I inspected them but did not think much of their efficiency. These doubts were confirmed when it was discovered that the store of cartridges they had brought with them were too large for their muskets. Fortunately my men had made a goodly number and they were of a proper size for their muskets—so I served out ammunition to the men placed on picket duty. We felt safer and work was resumed till one morning my store keeper informed me that some lead had been stolen during the previous night. An extra picket was placed over the lead stores, but still every night lead was stolen. One of my men an old sergeant took upon himself to watch, and one morning reported to me that these Turkish soldiers were the thieves and that if their tents were searched the stolen lead would be found there.

I immediately ordered the parade of all these Turkish soldiers in marching order.

Their commanding officer did not like this but I insisted and when all the men were in their ranks I took this officer into the tents lifted the boards and discovered the stolen lead. *Facts* were stubborn things, the officer begged I would not report it, but I told him I should certainly do so and ordered him and his men immediately to march back to Chanak

Kalehsi. Of course I reported this and the reasons for it to head quarters, begging for some English troops.

In the meantime my men had to resume their picket duties. Early one morning I was on the watch and perceived the head of a mounted column coming down the mountain. I ordered all hands to the redoubt I had built. The approaching column when on the plain formed into line and with shouts came gallopping down towards my camp.

When they had arrived at what I thought a proper distance I gave the order for my fellows to fire thro' the loop holes between the rolls of felt, behind which the party was concealed. The enemy did not look for such a reception so they wheeled and rode off into the country again to continue their plunderings there.

The whole country was roused—a detachment of English troops was sent to me, the very day before your dear "Ama" and your dear Father arrived in the Dardanelles—I went in my boat to meet them and brought them to my camp. That very night we had an alarm but the British sentries were on the alert and the enemy retired. These men by their cruelties and plunderings had aroused the natives of the country and they were nearly all killed. I got the arms of one of their number—2 daggers, a brace of pistols and a sword, which I have to this day. A memento of this exciting affair.

Work there went on briskly, and I was very happy in the society of my loved ones—from whom I had been so long separated.

[67]

Your dear Father was appointed by the War Office as my assistant, and a most useful one I found him.

Some months after this and just as we had some 1600 patients in the Hospital, I received notice from the War office that negotiations for peace with Russia were in hand and that I was to stop all works at the Hospital. I did not like that my 150 Army Works Corps fellows should be turned loose with nothing to do, fearing they might get into mischief; so I camped them out on the plains of Troy,—determining to commence some excavations at the Necropolis.

My men did not like this at first, but an extra pint of stout per day which I ordered for them partly reconciled them to it—and by & bye when we came on ancient tombs, sarcophagi, amphorae &c they got much interested and worked away with great zest.

We found a great many things,—vases, armlets, anklets, earrings &c.

I detached a section of my men to Illium Novum, and put them to excavate there.

I found the ruins of a temple, the Corinthian capital of one of the columns, evidently shaken down by an earthquake, was the most beautiful piece of carving in white marble I ever saw. It weighed over 3 tons—we had some difficulty in getting it out of the hole in which we discovered it. There were no roads to the place along which a cart could be brought to convey it away—so I was forced to roll it up the mound under which I had found it, set it up on end, and to my great regret leave it there.

[68]

We came upon the walls of a house very near this spot. The plaster was still on the walls, and we could see the colour which had been used upon the plaster. We dug down a little deeper and came upon the tessellated pavement of a room. We cleared the whole area of the room. In the centre of the room was a large oval tessellated picture,—the subject a Boar hunt, beautifully worked in variously tinted marbles. While I was gazing at this work of art, and determining to cut out this picture and bring it away at whatever cost I received despatches from the Hospital which required that I and my men should march back there at once. I ordered all the earth and material we had excavated from this room to be thrown in again—determining that I would soon return & get the picture.

There were a good many Greeks about looking at what we were doing.

That night we marched back to Renkioi. About a fortnight afterwards I organized a small party and went out to the spot to exhume & bring away the picture.

When we arrived at the spot, you may imagine my disgust and anger on finding that some one had been there and forestalled me—the picture had been cut out and was gone. As the next best thing I cut out and brought away a piece of the bordering round the room. This ended my explorations at Troy. All the things I had found I had carefully packed in boxes—intending to bring them to England on my return there.

Very soon after this peace was declared and I got orders to advertise and sell every thing at the

Hospital by public auction, and the Dardanelles Consul Calvert was ordered to assist me in this. While organizing this I felt still anxious to recover the inlaid picture, I offered £5 reward for it. Soon afterwards I was told that a Greek Priest in a village some miles away could tell me something about it. I made an expedition to this village and found out the Priest. At first he was very shy but after my offering him £10 if he could get it for me, he relaxed a little and said he would show it to me. We went together to his church and there immediately in front of the High Altar was my picture let into the tile pavement.

Anything so incongruous could not be imagined. The picture of a boar Hunt in such a sacred place!

But there it was. The Priest promised to do his best to get the parties who had placed it there as an offering to agree to its being removed and handed over to me. He also promised that I should hear from him in a few days.

These few days elapsed when I received a communication from him, that he had done his best to get it, but it was much as his life was worth to allow it to be removed. Having been placed where it was as a votive offering, it became according to their notions, sacred. So ended that affair.

Meanwhile advertizing placards had been printed and sent in every direction. I took steamer up to Constantinople, went to the Grand Viziar and tried my best to persuade the Turkish Government to purchase the whole of the Buildings and appliances as they stood, showing what a splendid military school might be established there.

It was all no use. The Turkish officials were so dilatory and apathetic I could make no impression upon them, and I came away in disgust.

The week for the auction arrived. A short time previously a great fire at Salonica had rendered some thousands of the inhabitants houseless—so a deputation came over to purchase some of the wards of the Hospital, which were of timber, for housing these houseless ones. When the Tallal or Auctioneer commenced his labours the bidding for these wards was brisk, and they realised good prices. Day after day the sale went on—much to my satisfaction— till at last we came to what I called the machinery department, a list of which was published. I valued the lot in my own mind at £10,000. The bidding for this lot was very slow—it reached £450—and the Tallal kept calling out this sum for a long while, still no advance—and he had orders to knock down no lot without a signal from me.

I went to him and asked him to point me out the bidder of this amount, which he did, and I at once recognized the Greek, who was a sort of agent for Calvert the British Consul. I sought out Calvert in the crowd and remonstrated with him. I knew that all the people of the Dardanelles held Calvert in such dread that they dared not bid against him. Calvert said "Come, Brunton, knock this lot down; you know your orders are very strict: you must sell everything by public auction." I remonstrated with him and said I certainly would not knock it down for any such price, if he wanted the lot he must boldly bid something near its value. The shouting of the Tallal still went on. At last Calvert, calling me aside, said "Look here Brunton, knock it down and I will give you an undertaking that you shall have half the profits." I was staggered that such a proposition as this should come from a British Consul. "No Calvert," said I, "You have the wrong pig by the ear this time." I called out at once to the Tallal: " £1000 for this lot. I buy it in." Calvert was furious. I immediately determined what I would do and sat down and wrote Calvert an order to send down a steamer that night to take me up to Constantinople, determining to try & get vessels to take this lot of things back to England where I knew I could sell them for a vast deal more than had been offered at the auction.

 I summoned your dear Father, told him what I was going to do and instructed him to muster all the Army Works Corps fellows and carefully to pack up all the unsold articles.

That evening the steamer came down and took me to Constantinople. I immediately went to Lord Lyons who was in charge of the despatch home of troops and stores.

He received me very kindly. I told him the whole history of this transaction and showed him my Orders from the War office. I told him I wanted 2 good ships to take these stores and my 150 men to England. He shook his head at first but on reflection he said that there were 2 East India men, the "Cœur de Lion" and the "Rajusthan" lying then in the Golden Horn—in excess of the transport he required and they were going home in ballast.

"I will order you these if you like but recollect I take none of the responsibility of your breaking War office orders."

"I will take all that my Lord", said I, "and I am infinitely obliged to you."

He gave me the orders, and I delivered the orders to the Captains of the two ships—who were delighted—they were quite tired of lying in the Golden Horn.

I ordered them down to Renkioi at once, went on board my own steamer and was at Renkioi the next morning. I found that in my absence the packing had gone on vigourously.

In 2 days my two East India men arrived and we soon loaded them. I put your father in charge sending my 150 Army Works Corps fellows as passengers under his command.

They sailed. I took your dear "Ama" up to Constantinople to show it her, we went up in one of H.M. Troopships, and after a few days inspection of the Golden Horn, the "sweet waters" of Europe and Asia, and a row up the Bosphorus in a caique, calling on and, by invitation, lunching with the now famous General Gordon (then a Captain) we took passages to Trieste in one of the Austrian Lloyds steamers determined to return to England overland.

We left the beautiful scenery of the Bosphorus with regret, in the Dardanelles we passed the Renkioi Hospital scite, bidding it farewell; It was now a completely deserted spot only recognizable by an enormous board I had put up, early in the occupation, having the name "Renkioi Hospital" painted thereon.

Our voyage was a delightful one, the scenery as

we passed thro the numerous islands of the Archipelago perfectly enchanting.

We stopped off Athens to land mails but were not allowed to go ashore ourselves, cholera having made its appearance there. Past the Ionian islands we steamed, and arrived at Trieste.

Great was our desire to have gone across to Venice but we had a long land journey before us and I was anxious to get to London before my vessels arrived at Spithead, where they were to call for orders.

From Trieste to Vienna, Dresden, Frankfort, Cologne & Brussels, at each of which places we stopped and visited the picture galleries and other sights, enjoying ourselves immensely.

From Brussels we went to Antwerp—a fine old place & most interesting. Here resided your dear Ama's old nurse, for your Grandmama was born in Antwerp, and in letters from home, we had been particularly enjoined to call and see the old body.

We sailed for the Thames in the "Baron Osy". On our arrival I proceeded to the War office at once to report myself and my doings. I found my old acquaintance Mr Milton there.

When I reported that I had departed from my instructions and that two cargoes of stores were on their way to England—he got furious and walked up and down the room, blowing me up with the greatest severity. I had anticipated all this and calmly waited till he had tired himself. He told me that the stores brought home had filled every warehouse The Government could engage, there was no place to store what was coming in my ships—that I was responsible for a grave breach of orders &c &c.

I begged of him to leave the matter in my hands and allow me to finish the work that had been entrusted to me. I left him, jumped into a cab and drove to the Tower. I enquired from the authorities there what, if any, of the warehouses the Government had engaged were yet vacant. After a long search he told me that Nos 35 & 36 Victoria Docks were yet unoccupied.

I asked him to reserve them for me. This he said he could not do without orders from the War Office. "Will you keep them for me for an hour" said I. This he promised to do.

Into my cab I rushed and back to the War office. "Mr Milton" said I "Nos 35 & 36 Victoria docks are vacant I want your authority to occupy them." "I dont believe it" said he. "Telegraph to the Tower and enquire" said I. This he at once did & the reply came back "that these warehouses were vacant but that I had applied for them".

On this he could do nothing less than engage them for me. Thus I scored well off him and was satisfied. Immediately I telegraphed orders to Spithead for the ships on arrival to come on to the Thames and take up these two berths in Victoria Docks. A few days of rather impatient waiting and I received a telegram from your dear Father that he and the two ships had safely arrived at Spithead, had rec^d their orders, and were off to the Thames. He was coming to join me by rail. This was good news which made us most thankful.

We got news of the arrival of the ships in the docks and were down to meet them. My Army Works Corps fellows were in splendid order and condition having been living on board like fighting cocks.

They went to work with a will and we unloaded the ships, without a days demurrage—so that in fact these stores had come home for nothing. I put my men to unpack and clean up every thing. I had now to go to work and dispose of these stores which consisted of a very heterogeneous mass of things.

A few days afterwards the Medical Department of the Government advertised for tenders for 500 water closets and a number of Lavatories for Netley Military Hospital, which was then in course of erection. In my own name I sent in a tender and sample. As I had purchased all these articles I knew what the wholesale price was or ought to be.

My satisfaction was great when, in due course, my Tender was accepted. I sent in the lot and acknowledgement came for the receipt of the same. Sales went briskly on, and at last I had only remaining 60 ventilating fans which had been sent out for the purpose of ventilating the Hospital wards. I could not find a customer for these, and was despairing when one morning I saw an article in the newspapers stating that the stoke-holes in Her Majesty's Gun boats had proved so deficient in ventilation that the stokers had struck work.

Here was a chance for me. I went at once to Sir

Baldwin Walker the first lord of the Admiralty. I told him, I had read that paragraph, and I should be glad to know if the facts stated therein were true —for I had invented a plan for ventilating stoke holes which I felt sure would be a success.

He replied that all was true, and that the Admiralty would be very glad to adopt my scheme if it were successful. I asked for permission to erect my machinery in any of the Gun boats then lying at Woolwich, and requested Sir Baldwin to appoint a Commission to inspect and report to him upon the success or otherwise of my scheme. To this Sir Baldwin at once assented and he ordered me to go down to Woolwich and see the Engineer of the Dockyard, select a gun boat on which to try the experiment; at the same time he appointed a Commission to report upon it. You may be sure I was not long before I was at Woolwich and with the Engineer inspecting the various Gun boats. "Give me the worst of them" said I—and very soon the worst was selected.

I told him I must cut a hole in the deck; to this he demurred but on my undertaking that should the ventilation scheme prove a failure I would personally be responsible for all cost in repairing the deck, he assented.

A day for the trial was appointed—and I sent down one of these fans in a large wooden case marked "Brunton's improved machinery for Ventilation". My men went with it cut the hole in the deck and fixed the Fan, attaching to it, a hollow tube of canvas, called a winsail, which extended from the Fan down into the stoke hole to within about 3 feet of the floor.

Everything was ready the night before the trial in presence of the Commission.

We all met on board. "Now Gentlemen," said I "you must be good enough to come down with me into the Stoke hole." This proposition did not at first suit the tastes of these Gentlemen who, with their portly figures, nice clean black clothes, and stiff limbs (for they were all elderly) did not much approve of descending the narrow almost vertical ladders, which they knew led down to the dirty, dark regions below.

I insisted however upon the absolute necessity of this and the descent was made amidst a good deal of amusement at some of the party nearly sticking fast during the passage.

I had given orders to my men, that on a signal from me, they were to drive the Fan vigorously—and here I must tell you, that tho' the Fan on this trial was driven by hand eventually it was to be driven by a belt from the main shaft of the Engine. This of course I explained. We were all gathered below. I gave the signal, the windsail swelled out and a blast struck the floor of the stoke hole, creating a fearful dust causing much sneezing and making a pretty mess over all the nice black coats, not to mention the faces of us all.

One old gentleman approached the winsail, put down his head to look up it, wondering I suppose where the wind came from. Its force blew his hat off. They at once pronounced the *ventilation* perfect and begged me to stop it which I did. Amidst much merriment we, by degrees, scrambled on deck again and great was the laughter and joking at each others appearance. Amidst hearty congratulations on my success—promises of a favorable report and shaking of hands, we parted. Mr Anderson the Engineer to the Dock yard promised me that the report should reach Sir Baldwin Walker without loss of time. In a couple of days I called again on Sir Baldwin, and was received with hearty congratulations on the complete success of my scheme. He asked how soon I could deliver some fans at Woolwich, & at what price. I replied I could deliver 60 in a fortnight and the price was £15 each (their original cost). He gave me the order for this number at this price. I delivered them, getting the formal receipt for the same. This fortunate sale enabled me to close my a/c sales, which amounted to between 11 and £12,000.

I went and presented it to Mr Milton, much to his astonishment both at the amount and more particularly that I had sold so many things back to the Government. This was easy as the several departments are ignorant of, and do not interfere with each other's transactions.

I had taken advantage of this, and by selling and delivering the articles in my own name, had made the matter easier and less likely to incur opposition. It was clear that I had saved the Government over £11,000. Mr Milton said that I deserved some substantial recognition of this and he would recommend that I should be paid a Commission of 5 % on the sum I had saved. In parting from him and thanking him I could not help reminding him of the scolding he had given me for disobeying orders. I left him & considered I had certainly scored again in my transactions with him.

A few days afterwards I received a letter from the War Office signed by Mr Milton requesting me to call there next morning at 10 o/c as a mistake had been discovered in my accounts! This was serious. I had been most careful with the accounts, and could not imagine where a mistake could lie.

I passed almost a sleepless night—but presented myself before Mr Milton at the time named. "Well Mr Milton" said I "your letter has made me very uneasy & deprived me of my nights sleep—what is this error and where is it." "A mistake in cash accounts is a very serious matter Sir" says Mr Milton and on he went preaching a sort of sermon on this most unpleasant subject. I interrupted him demanding to know the particulars, but again he resumed his discourse, but with a sort of twinkle in his eye which made me think the matter was not of serious am^t at any rate.

At last he burst out laughing. "You have scored against me so many times, that I was determined to score one against you at any rate. The error is 2/- *in your favour.*" I felt at first very angry but at last could not help joining in the laughter with which his face and sides were convulsed. He told me the accounts had been passed—that he had done his best to get me the 5 per cent commission, but that they had presented me with £100 over and above my pay—accompanied by a handsome letter or testimonial from Lord Passmore who was Minister of War. Mr Milton paid me the money thus due to me including the 2/- which had caused so much amusement as well as anxiety.

I presented the Trojan relics to the British

Museum, the Authorities there sent Panici the
Curator of Antiquities to inspect the collection. He
ticketted all except one signet engraved stone which
I reserved as a memento of the pleasant hours I had
spent there. Panici was very anxious for it—as he
said they had no example of the figure engraved on
it. I had it set as a ring—which I have worn ever
since. Some day dear Jack it shall be yours.

Thus ended my Crimean career.

I had had many hardships to go through, much
anxiety and hard work, some dangers, but many
many mercies which made me very thankful. It had
also added much to my knowledge of men and things
which I hope and believe have been useful to me
ever since. I look back upon them with much gratitude and interest.

VII

THE sale of these stores had occupied nearly
four months it was now the end of March
1856. While it was going on, I had proposals
made to me for employment in India. One was to
take charge of the construction of Railways in the
Island of Ceylon—another to take the superin-
tendance of the erection of 2 large Iron bridges
about to be erected by the East India Railway Coy
under Mr George Turnbull, and the third a proposal that I should go out as Chief Engineer of the
Scinde Railway between Karachi and Kotru on the
Indus. These were all very flattering offers. I
earnestly prayed for guidance from above in making
my choice. It fell upon the last I have mentioned
and on the 7th June 1856 I received intimation of
my being appointed Chief Engineer and your dear
Father Assistant Engineer of the Scinde Railway.

We were to proceed to India in the autumn and
in the meantime I was to make drawings of the

Buildings and machinery required for a large Engine repairing and erecting Shop to be erected at Karachi.

Mr Andrew (now Sir Willm Patrick Andrew) the chairman had laid out a scheme for a complete line of Railway from Karachi to Delhi on the East Indian Railway.

The construction of the Punjab section from Mooltan to Lahore & Amritzur was then going forward, and my brother was in charge as Chief Engineer.

Mr Jarrow was the Consulting Engineer of the Company here in England.

I was very busy, I made visits to several of our largest Locomotive Engine establishments in England—and got out drawings which were approved and sanctioned. In July I went and engaged passages for myself, your dear Grandmama and your Father, by the P and O steamers, then sailing from Marseilles to Alexandria—and from Suez to Bombay. A few days after this the astounding news of the Indian Mutiny arrived. All officers on leave in England were ordered to return to their Regiments. I feared for the private cabin the P and O people had booked for the accommodation of myself and your Grandmama.

I went there to enquire and they assured me that pressed as they were for room—my cabin which had been booked before the news arrived should be kept for me.

During my Crimean experiences I had made many very pleasant acquaintances & friendships, among the latter was that of Dr Goodeve and his wife. When he heard that I was going out to India Dr Goodeve came to see me. Having been in India many years, I consulted him on many points on which I was ignorant. He gave me much good advice—one item was, never to drink the water from the country wells, but to stick to Soda water manufactured from known good, pure water. I treasured all his advice but this in particular as he laid such stress upon it.

Late in August 1856 we left for Marseilles overland and embarked there. Sir Hugh Rose (now Lord Strathnairn) and Colonel Wyndham were amongst the passengers, I made the acquaintance of both. We had a pleasant voyage to Alexandria calling at Malta where we landed and had time to visit the famous Cathedral of St John.

Usually the whole area of the nave is covered with thick matting to prevent the damage which peoples boots and shoes would do to the tesselated tombstones with which the floor is covered. Here were buried the Knights of St John who as Crusaders fought and died in the Holy Land. Each tombstone bore an elaborate Coat of Arms—in coloured marbles.

The matting is only taken up on special festivals —the day we were there was one of them and the sight was most interesting. The Cathedral itself is constructed with plain Norman semicircular arches and the effect is solemn and very impressive.

We arrived at Alexandria—there was no railway then to run one down to Suez, we had to travel by the old caravan route. This was accomplished in a sort of box on a pair of wheels—holding six persons inside, drawn by 4 mules—a fearfully primitive and uncomfortable vehicle.

Of all the party crossing to Suez, we were the last, arriving at Suez, at about 1 o'c in the morning.

The Hotel, kept by a Portuguese was full, and more than full. With great difficulty I got your grandmama into a sitting room where she found the floor covered with ladies, who with some difficulty made room for her to lie down amongst them and the children. The fact was the Steamer had just arrived from Bombay loaded with ladies and their families fleeing from India on account of the Mutiny. They brought most harrowing tales of the cruelties which the natives had practised and were practising up Country in India. Your dear Father and I had to lie down in one of the passages—our hand bags for our pillows. Next morning we went on board the Steamer. The heat was fearful.

We sailed down the Red Sea, at about the same pace as the wind. The smoke of the vessel hung in a black canopy over our heads and we all lay on deck at night. The cabins were perfectly unbearable. Most thankful were we when we arrived at Aden, and after coaling left the Red Sea behind us.

I retain very pleasant recollections of the conversations I had with Sir Hugh Rose, and General Wyndham. The latter was the life of the ship—going about from group to group—and with his amusing anecdotes keeping us all cheerful. When off Bombay, the Captain of the Steamer (Captain Burns) had to signal to know whether all was quiet

& safe for us to enter the Harbour. Such was the dread entertained that Bombay might be in possession of the Mutineers. The reply was favorable and we steamed into the most magnificent harbour you can conceive.

We landed and went in search of accomodation at the Hotels—every place full to overflowing. The Monsoon was not over and deluges of rain were falling. At last we took refuge in a building, no better than a cowshed, in the corner of the compound of one of the Hotels. However here also was Sir Hugh for a time only—for his arrival being known to the Governor of Bombay he was quickly summoned to high quarters. What were we to do? I at last thought of an old acquaintance of mine, Mr James Berkeley, who was Chief Engineer to the Great Indian Peninsular Railway and resided in Bombay. I wrote him a pencil note detailing our position and asking for his advice as to getting apartments somewhere.

My Messenger quickly returned bringing the kindest of notes telling me at once to come, bag and baggage, up to his Bungalow.

This invitation, as you may imagine, was not declined, we hired buggies, for it was pouring, and were soon in hospitable quarters.

Mr & Mrs Berkeley being most kind, next day I reported myself to Lord Elphinstone the Governor, who forbad me going up to Karachi at present. I shall never forget the gloom and despondency on all European's faces. The Massacre at Cawnpore, and the loss of life at other places had struck terror and dismay throughout India. Bombay was crowded

with refugees from the interior most of the garrison
there had been sent to assist at the siege of Delhi—
which was the head quarters of the Mutineers—and
the roughs or "Budmashus" as they are called were
only waiting to hear of success on the mutineers
side at Delhi to pillage and probably murder the
Europeans in Bombay.

One night while I was waiting in Bombay
Berkeley & I sat up rather late chatting, and your
dear Grandmama had retired to bed.

When I went up to our room she was fast asleep,
the mosquito curtains tucked in all round the bed.
When ready for bed I quietly lifted up one side of
the muslin curtains, got in to bed, and laid myself
down to sleep, having again tucked in the curtains.
I had hardly dosed when I was roused by a feeling
of something or somebody touching the hair on the
top of my head. (I had some there in those days!)
I did not move, but waited a repetition of the sensation. It soon came, I made a sudden snatch at
whatever might be there, rose, and looked for it,
when I saw an enormous Bandakut rat scuttling off.
Knowing that the mosquito curtains would not allow
of this unwelcome nocturnal visitor getting away—
I roused your Grandmama, and I began chasing the
rat round and round. The night light or Butti as it
is called, which we always burn at nights in India,
enabling us to see our intruder quite distinctly.
After some unsuccessful attempts I at last caught
the rascal in the bight of a sheet. When I got fairly
hold of him I gave him a squeeze and twist which
fairly broke his backbone. He was dead, and I
tossed him out on to the floor, intending to take his
dimensions next morning.

We went to sleep again. I dreamt that I saw the animal running away—I woke, and looked out. There he lay as I had tossed him out and looking at my watch, saw that he had been there 2 hours. Next morning he was gone. On telling the story at breakfast Mr Berkeley said that no doubt his comrades had carried him away to their lair and devoured him.

These rats are very large and destructive. I am sure my victim had ears as large as my thumb.

At the recommendation of the landlady at the Hotel, in the shed of which we had passed several hours of misery before Mr Berkeley's hospitable offer arrived, I had engaged a native servant who was to be butler or head servant in my domestic establishment. His papers appeared quite satisfactory—so I handed him over charge of my luggage. 2 days afterwards I missed 7 English sovereigns taken from one of my boxes. I discharged him, and through Berkeley's help I succeeded in securing a Goanese—a native of Goa which is a Portuguese settlement in India. He was very black—blacker than the ordinary natives of Hindustan—but he was a Roman Catholic and therefore a Christian. I mention this because this man turned out a most faithful servant & remained my butler throughout my Indian experiences. You may hear more of him by & bye.

The Governor of Bombay was very anxious to keep up the spirits of the Europeans there, and consequently kept up his 2 Government house dinner parties each week. I had the honour of invitations.

After I had been a fortnight in Bombay all my party (your dear Grandmama, your dear Father, and I) were at one of these gatherings.

Behind each visitors chair stood a Government House native Servant in Livery, and lately it had been noticed that all the native servants had become sulky and inclined to disobey orders, no doubt hoping and expecting that we should fail in the attack and siege of Delhi, the stronghold of the Mutineers, who as they represented were to free India from the rule of England. In the middle of dinner a telegram was placed in the Governor's hands. He opened and read it. Then rising exclaimed—Ladies & Gentlemen, listen to this "Delhi has fallen and is now in our hands". When this announcement was made the expression on the faces of the row of Native servants fell in a most wonderful manner, I could not help noticing it. It was like shutting down Venetian blinds.

The assembled company rose and cheered long and loudly—the ladies waving their handkerchiefs while tears of joy and thankfulness rolled down their cheeks. As you may suppose very little more was eaten. Extra Champaign was ordered in, and the health of Lawrence drank with loud cheers.

Here was the backbone of the Mutiny broken. When I went to bid His Lordship good night he greeted me "Now Brunton you may be off to Karachi as soon as you like."

This news was very consoling & encouraging & next day I booked passages by the outgoing Steamer for Karachi, where after a tediously long passage we arrived.

We established ourselves in a Bungalow near the Artillery Barracks, and I entered on my duties as Chief Engineer of the Scinde Railway.

One of my first duties, after mustering the Engineering Staff and inspecting all the plans & sections which my predecessor Mr Wells had made, was to start out and march along the line thus laid out, with a view to improve it if possible.

As it was then the cold season, as we in India call the winter, I at once organized the trip of inspection, which necessitated buying tents and camp equipage generally. I was of course quite ignorant of Indian ways (what is called a "Griffen") and had to depend very much upon the Butler I told you of. You can have no idea how much organization and preparation such an expedition requires. I had to engage 12 Tent-pitchers. I found a Beloocher who had very good testimonials & engaged him as "Tindal" or Foreman of the Tent-pitchers, Camel men &c. He brought to me about 20 Beloochers (his countrymen) to select the Tent-pitchers from. A finer lot of men I never saw—they were all dressed in white, not one amongst the lot less than 6 feet and 1 inch in height, some 6 feet 4 inches. The Beloochers all wear their hair long—it is quite black and a great length, kept scrupulously clean, oiled, plaited, and bound round their heads, mixed with strips of Turkey Red cloth. This forms a handsome and excellent head-covering or Turban for resisting the heat of the sun. They claim to be one of the lost ten tribes of Israel, but are Mahomedans now.

Then I had Camels to engage—one Riding Camel for myself and the rest to carry the tents and baggage. I was more at home when selecting a horse. When all was ready I left my dear ones in Karachi and started on my march. Before taking you along with me in this first of my expeditions into the jungle I must tell you of the very narrow escape of the European inhabitants of Karachi, from becoming victims to the Mutineers.

Sir Bartle Frere was Commissioner in Scinde, General Scott was in command of the Military stationed in Karachi, which at the time I speak of and about a fortnight before I had arrived there, consisted of 2 weak Companies of the 2nd European Regiment, the 14th Native Regt, the 21st Bengal Native Regt and one Battery of Artillery. No symptom had appeared of either of these Native regiments being mutinously disposed. All seemed safe and quiet.

Sir Bartle and the General had gone out one Saturday to spend Sunday at their country Bungalows, at a place called Clifton about 5 miles away, leaving the Military charge of the Cantonment in the hands of Brigadier Louth. One night about 11 o'c a subidar, or noncommissioned officer of the 21st Regt came to the Brigadier's bungalow, and addressing the soldier on guard, asked to see the Brigadier.

The sentry replied that he was in bed asleep and must not be disturbed. The subidar was peremptory and said he *must* see him. So the sentry at last called one of the Brigadier's servants and sent him in to tell his master that the Subidar wanted very much to speak to him.

The Brigadier replied that the Subidar had better

come to him next morning. But when this message was given the Subidar became more peremptory than ever—so another message was sent in to the Brigadier, who, putting on his dressing gown, came out to see what all this meant. The Subidar asked to speak to him in private. He then said "Brigadier Sahib, you have several times been very kind to me, so I have come to tell you that the 21st Regiment are going to mutiny at 12 o'c tonight, the whole of the Cantonment has been mapped out, and men told off to each division who are to murder every European and pillage the Bungalows." This was startling news. The Brigadier at once sent off orders to the 2 companies of the 2nd Europeans to get under arms at once without sound of bugle or drum. The same message was also sent to the 14th Native Infantry, whom the Subidar had stated were not in any way connected with the movement contemplated by the 21st and that the whole were to march down at once and take up certain positions which commanded the barracks of the 21st. The Battery of Artillery were also ordered to get ready to galop down, on a rocket signal being fired, and to take up certain positions. With admirable celerity all this was done—and at about 5 minutes to 12 the Brigadier at the head of the troops ordered the 21st Regt. to turn out. This at first they refused to do altho' their European officers had gone amongst them and endeavoured to bring them to a sense of their duty. However some of the 21st had looked out and seen that the guns were placed commanding their barracks and the portfires were lighted, all ready for action. The Brigadier then took out his watch and warned them that if in 5 minutes they did not obey his orders to turn out he would open fire upon them—they reluctantly turned out and formed

[92]

up in the Barrack square. The order was then given "Pile Arms".

This was obeyed—"Retire" was then given, and immediately the 2nd Europeans went in and collected all the arms—putting them into carts, which had been sent for, and sending them away to the Arsenal. On calling the roll of the 21st it was discovered that 27 men were missing, they had slipped away & got off.

As soon as it was day the police "puggers" (men who are educated to track people by the mark of their footsteps) were put on their tracks and I may tell you now that in about 3 weeks time all these 27 mutineers were caught and brought back to Karachi. A court martial was held upon them and they were all blown away from guns. As the Subidar had told the Brigadier, a map of the Cantonment was found marked out as he had described.

Was not this a most Providential escape? The 21st Regt was disbanded, and no regiment of that number has since been formed.

The men of it were all Bengalese of a high Brahmin caste. The 14th Regt had been recruited from all castes, and not a breath of suspicion against their fidelity was ever whispered.

But now I am on my march up the country towards Kotru and Hydrabad. You must know that on the average we cannot do more than about 10 miles per day, because ones servants and attendants have to walk it. During the night the day tents are sent forward & pitched ready for the Sahib's arrival early next morning. The sleeping tents following during the day. Surrounded by natives, in whom no great confidence was reposed at that time we few Europeans moved about armed. I had a brace of loaded revolvers in my belt and a sword by my side —a sword I had purchased when before leaving Karachi I had joined, as an officer, a Volunteer Corps which had been hastily formed.

On the morning of the 5th day after leaving Karachi I and my party were approaching my camp which had been pitched in the neighbourhood of a village called Garra. We saw before us a very excited crowd of natives brandishing sticks and making a great noise. Not liking the looks of this, I halted the party and sent my Moonshee (native interpreter) forward to ascertain what was the cause of this disturbance. He soon returned and told me that a mad wolf had bitten two of my men. We at once pushed forward. I found my Dhobi (washerman) was one of the sufferers and one of my tent pitchers was the other.

They told me that they had gone with my Butler into the bazaar of the village to purchase provisions and were returning along the street of the village the Dhobi carrying in his hand a tin can of milk. On passing a stack of timber the wolf sprung out upon them, seized the hand of the Dhobi in which he was carrying the can, crushed the can and very severely lacerated the poor fellow's hand.

The tent-pitcher had been knocked down but not bitten. I at once put a tight bandage round the upper part of the Dhobi's arm, and placed his hand in a vessel of warm water to encourage the bleeding.

I went into my tent and took off my belt and arms—
and seeing my "Syce", or groom, dressing my
horse under the shade of a tree, across the sandy
plain lying between my tent and the edge of the
thick jungle, I thought I would walk across to have
a look at my nag. When about half way across this
sandy plain, I heard a fearful yell evidently from the
jungle, immediately afterwards I saw the wolf rush
out and make for my horse. The Syce saw him
coming and when very near he threw the curry
comb at him with great force, striking him on the
head. This turned the mad brute who then came at
full speed towards me.

I had nothing to defend myself with, not a stone
amongst the dry sand, & not even a curry comb like
the syce. I sung out loudly to the people in the camp
to let loose the 2 dogs, belonging to one of my staff,
I waved my big sun-topi and made loud demonstrations. The brute I suppose did not like the appearance of them, changed his course a little, passed me
within 5 or 6 yards, and made for my camp, he was
met by the 2 dogs; one of them weighing at least
25 lbs he seized by the back, shook him fiercely,
tossed him, fearfully bitten, over his shoulder and
kept on his course. He went right through the camp,
fortunately biting no one, away along the path
alongside the jungle. The cry there was, Arm,
mount and after him! This was responded to by a
few of my people. I enquired about the yell I had
heard when crossing the "maidan" or sandy plain
and discovered that it had proceeded from one of
my men who was gathering fire wood in the jungle,
and who had been frightfully bitten in the face,
almost destroying one eye.

I had learnt something about doctoring while out amongst the Hospitals during the Crimean War—but this was a case beyond me altogether. So I ordered a couple of camels to be got ready and despatched the Dhobi and the other wounded man to the Hospital at Karachi—and here I may as well say that the Dhobi got all right again, returned to my service and remained with me for years afterwards. The other poor fellow four months afterwards died from hydrophobia altho the wounds in his face had quite healed.

That, on this occasion, I had had a very narrow escape was evident. A kind Providence had watched over me, most thankful was I at the time and am so whenever this stirring incident comes across my memory.

In India a record is kept of all fatalities arising from attacks of wild beasts, snakes &c—on this occasion the return gave 12 men bitten, of whom 10 died, and a large number of cattle. The brute was hunted down and killed by the natives, the day after our interview with him.

This was far from a pleasant opening to my camping career.

Two marches further, and I was halting on Sunday as I always did, when in the afternoon I was startled by hearing a horse galloping into my camp. I sent out to enquire, what was the matter—my Moonshee returned bringing with him a scared looking fellow, who stated that the mutiny had broken out afresh in Karachi—that all the Europeans were killed, and that he only had escaped and was on his way to Hydrabad.

The fellow was a Eurasian and could speak a little English, so I commenced to cross examine him. He contradicted himself in several important particulars, and tho' much startled by such news I felt sure it could not be so bad as he at first had represented. As you will recollect I had left your dear Father and his mother behind me in Karachi—and if half what this fellow had told me was correct, what was their fate? I ordered my riding camel at once, and as the sun was setting started to ride through the night the 56 miles which separated me from them. I could not rest till I knew the truth. I mounted, and jog, jog, jog—throughout the night at the rate of 6 miles an hour we travelled wearily on, my fears alternating with hopes and prayers. Without a stop for rest or refreshment we arrived at sunrise at my Bungalow and much astonished the dear occupants.

The camel, the driver and myself pretty well exhausted, for myself all was repaid by finding your dear Ama and your father quite safe and well. On enquiry I found that there had been an alarm, almost groundless when investigated. Your grandmama had heard of it and felt somewhat nervous—but on retiring for the night her fears were lessened, by hearing the click of the billiard balls from the Artillery officers mess house, which as I before told you was close by our Bungalow. As soon as my camel and his driver were rested sufficiently I made the return journey to my camp—and without further startling adventures arrived at Kotru and Hydrabad —for the first time seeing the famous River Indus, on the navigation of which by a Flotilla of Steamers under my Engineering charge I was to be engaged.

On this journey I had marked out several places where improvements could be made in the course of the Line of Railway, a further inspection on my march back to Karachi confirmed this, and I at once divided out the line into districts and divisions, appointed an Engineer from my staff on each, and set them all to work to take levels and surveys.

Another march up and down the line accompanied by your Grandmama finished this cold season's work. Your dear Father had a division on the line. At the close of the cold season all my Staff came into Karachi from the districts and were engaged during the hot season in plotting their work and making regular plans and sections.

It was during this hot season of 1858 that General Jacob being in Karachi, Sir Bartle Frere invited me to meet him and discuss general Railway communication between Karachi and Mooltan, up the Indus Valley, and particularly a line from Sukken to Jacobabad the founder of which important station General Jacob was. Your great Uncle, my brother William was then Chief Engineer of the Punjab Railway and had been instructed by our Company to make that survey, which he had done & the matter was under the consideration of the India House, at home and the Supreme Govt of India at Calcutta.

Bray the Contractor selected by the Scinde Railway Road, came out and in the cold season 1858–9, commenced work on the line. I and my Staff had much to do in watching these proceedings and trying to keep Bray right. After about 12 months work Bray failed to pay his men and "bolted"—leaving about 12,000 of his workmen unpaid.

These men were composed not only of Sindese but a large number came from Central Asia and were a very rough lot. Their credit for food with the Benyas (provision dealers) was stopped and rioting commenced all along the line. Troops were called out to protect property and the crisis was very serious. I at once went to my good friend Sir Bartle Frere for advice and assistance. Under a clause in the Contract I seized all Bray's plant. The payment of the men the arrears due to them was the important point.

The amount due was something like £14,000— I told Sir Bartle that if he would authorize the Govt. Treasury to advance me the money, I would organize a pay staff and satisfy the rioters.

To this he at once consented, I went off up the line and met a crowd of the poor fellows, who in fact were starving. I told them that if they would be quiet, I would pay them all the money due to them within a week. This announcement got them credit with the native Provision dealers and the rioting was at an end. I got the paysheets from Bray's Agent—arranged for my staff of Engineers to be the pay masters, and the men were paid off within the week. The question then arose How were the works to be carried on? After much discussion it was settled that I should carry them on departmentally, as it was termed, that is, with the aid of my Engineers and assistants I was to complete the works and was to be supplied with funds for so doing. This involved much harder work than we formerly had; but all my Engineers, at a meeting I convened, cheerfully undertook it, in the hope and expectation that the Company would, by a bonus or in some other way, recognize our services.

I found out that Bray had been employing his men on the day work system. This I at once abolished and put the whole on piece work—that is, a man or party of men were paid according to the amount of work they did, and there was no premium on idleness or loitering at their work.

This was resisted by the men at first, but finding I was firm, they gradually fell into my way and the work went on rapidly.

Your dear Father I placed to superintend the erection of the Bahrun Viaduct which was on Mr Taylor Warren's District. It was a very heavy piece of stone masonry work, and required constant attention and supervision which he gave it most thoroughly. Many were the prophecies in the neighbourhood that the first flood season would see the whole washed away—but many years have since passed and not one stone of the viaduct has been disturbed.

There was one point on the line called Dorbaji where a station was necessary. Whenever the Engineers of that District camped there, he and all his native followers, were certain to be down with fever and ague. This became so serious that I made a special journey to the place to try and find out the cause of it; all the other stations on the line were healthy enough.

When I arrived there I made the native, who brought water to the camp, to show me the place whence he obtained the water. He took me about $\frac{1}{2}$ a mile into the jungle and showed me a small pond of water, covered with green slime and filth—for the Buffaloes & other animals grazing in the Jungles came here to drink, having no other water in the neighbourhood.

Here then, was as I believed the source of all the mischief. I at once made a careful geological survey of the district in the neighbourhood of Dorbaji, and settled that by sinking a well at a certain place, not so far off as that fearful pond, I should find water.

At once men were put to work to sink a well. At a depth of about 40 feet they came upon a fine spring of water. Then I made them line the well with stone-work, making it a "pucka" well as it is called. On the surface I built over the well a sort of little temple —fixed a jack roll and bucket all well fastened to the place lest they should be stolen, and ordered that all water for the camps should be drawn from this well. The lazy native did not like the trouble of winding up the water from this depth, and I was obliged to go to work and drain the old pond so that they could not get water there. It was hard upon the buffaloes and cattle but it was necessary to secure good water for my people. After this Dorbaji was as healthy, if not more so than any other station on the line. Proof positive was thus obtained that bad con-taminated water is the main cause of fever and ague from which so many people, native & European, suffer in India.

On my frequent marchings up and down the line, I always left my Bungalow at Karachi under the charge of one of my confidential native servants.

On our return home for some two years, we had never missed anything from the Bungalow.

But once on my return I missed a walking cane—

one that I valued much, for it had been sent to me by my Brother in law, from Borneo where unhappily for his family he had died.

I immediately sent for the servant who had been in charge, and asked him where the cane was. He was staggered, and assured me he had no idea—he had never missed it. A general search was made, it could not be found; I was angry and vexed but saw no means of finding it. Nine months afterwards as your dear grandmama & I were making one of our early morning marches, about 70 miles from Karachi, we overtook a native walking thro' the jungles. I hailed him, as we always did then, and asked him who he was and where he was going. When, in response to my call he came up to my horse's side, what should I see in his hand but my long lost cane. "You have a nice stick there" said I. "Ay Sahib" said he, handing it up to me to look at "very nice cane". "You rascal it was you then who stole my cane, for it is mine and was stolen from my Bungalow at Karachi." He at once fell on his knees protesting his innocence and saying he had bought it for a rupee in the Bazaar at Karachi. This was possibly, nay probably, the fact. I made him tell me where he lived, who his father was &c. threatening him with arrest and punishment should I find he had told me a lie. Of course I carried off my cane in triumph at having found it, in so extraordinary and unlooked for a fashion.

I have not lost it since—it is now in the umbrella stand in the entrance hall, and some day shall be dear Jack's if he will promise me to take care of it, and sometimes think of its adventures.

A few miles away from Karachi there is a very curious place called "Muggur Pir". It is a small pond of water surrounded with palm trees and jungle. A very pretty place, as you will agree with me in thinking, if you will look at one or two photographs of it in my Album. They were taken by my brother Robert. But you will at once exclaim, what are these curious looking animals I see in the water and on the banks?

Well, these are alligators, who inhabit this pool. They are held sacred by a certain class of natives —and called "Muggurs". Certain priests, as they call them reside close by who feed these animals, with the offerings brought by devotees seeking help from some affliction. Goats, brought there alive, are the customary offerings. These are killed on the margin of the pool by the priest, who cuts the body of the victim up into small pieces. When this is done, at the top of his voice he calls out "Ow Ow" which means "Come Come". From the pool there issue the Muggurs, who approach the priest ranging themselves in a line at the water's edge—with their enormous mouths wide open. The priest goes along the line, throwing into the open jaws of each as he passes a portion of the goat. The portion is immediately crushed between their very powerful jaws, and away each one scuttles back into the pool again to enjoy his repast.

I have seen the complete head of a goat, horns and all, thrown into the mouth of one of these muggurs. One crunch and the whole head, horns and all are smashed. The old patriarch of these inhabitants of the pool is kept in an enclosed den separate from the rest. He is called the "King of the Muggurs" and is fed separately as becomes his rank. He is kept painted red (vermillion), he is of larger size than the rest and considered specially holy. What a fearful depth of superstition and ignorance! Visitors to the place out of curiosity are particularly requested in no way to interfere with the animals. One day two larky young officers went there, armed with 2 soda water bottles, full, but tied together with about 2 yards of cord.

When the priest began the feeding at one end of the line of muggurs, these two young men commenced at the other by each throwing a bottle into the open mouths of two adjacent animals. Crash went the bottles with an explosion, and into the pool went the muggurs each clutching his prize—great was the commotion under water, each muggur trying to swallow his portion but prevented by his neighbour at the other end of the cord, greatly to the amusement of the authors of this miserable trick. The priests complained to the Authorities and a severe reprimand followed, I believe accompanied by a fine, I think your verdict would be that it served them right.

But to go back to the progress of the Railway works. I had laid the line from Kiamari up to Karachi Town along the Napier mole when the first Locomotive arrived from England.

Our good friend Sir Bartle Frere, the Commissioner of Scinde was leaving for Calcutta, to become, I believe, a member of the Supreme Council there. He had held his position as Commissioner for many years and was respected and beloved by every class, whether European or native. On a certain day he was to sail from Kiamari, and we worked hard to get the Locomotive Engine ready to take him down thither, as a kind of opening of the Railway in which he had taken so much interest.

The natives of Scinde had never *seen* a Locomotive Engine, they had heard of them as dragging great loads on the lines by some hidden power they could not understand, therefore they feared them, supposing that they moved by some diabolical agency, they called them Shaitan (or Satan). During the Mutiny the Mutineers got possession of one of the East Indian Line Stations where stood several Engines. They did not dare to approach them but stood a good way off and threw stones at them!

When I got out my Locomotive for trial the Karachi natives were astounded.

I had, at that time, no Railway carriages, so to convey Sir Bartle and Lady Frere down to Kiamari, I was obliged to convert common Railway goods trucks into accommodation for them, by extemporizing wooden seats, and rigging up cloth awnings. The morning came for Sir Bartle's departure. The whole population of the District had thronged in, to witness his embarkation and show their sorrow at his leaving. The gathering could not number less than 60 or 70,000, who were gathered all along the line of Railway, a distance of about 3 miles.

I drove the Engine myself of course at a slow speed—the natives thronging all round, I was fearful of some accident. At last I thought I would frighten them away, so I blew the Engine Steam

Whistle loudly. Instantly they all rushed back from the "Demon"—falling over one another, much to our amusement. I could liken it to nothing but the action of a scythe in a crop of standing corn. At last we reached Kiamari, and the farewell of Sir Bartle to the assembled mass was most pathetic.

The natives, most of them on their knees, crying and howling; and thus departed a man, who had won his way into the affections of all, by his kindness, his justice and his earnest endeavours to promote the prosperity of all under his rule.

Here I may tell you an anecdote of him, when, shortly after his leaving Scinde he was made Governor of the Bombay Presidency, where extensive Railway works were in progress particularly at the Bhore Ghant, on the Great Indian Peninsular Railway under my good old friend James Berkeley. It had become notorious that the European Foremen or Gangers employed by the Contractors for the works, used to strike and otherwise illuse the native workmen. This had come to Sir Bartle's ears, and he issued a Government order, that any Ganger or European striking a native should be instantly dismissed from the works, and forfeit his return passage to England which, in their original engagement, was guaranteed. The order was printed and circulated throughout the works.

One day Sir Bartle and Mr Ellis (now Sir Barrow Ellis) were travelling by carriage from Bombay towards Poonah through the Bhore Ghant.

The road was very steep, so they left their carriage and struck down off the high road to a place where the Railway works were being carried on and a large number of natives were at work.

They approached the party, and encountered a big brawny navvy, an Englishman who appeared to be superintending operations. Sir Bartle addressed him in his mild kind way.

"Well, my good man, you appear to be the manager here."

"Yes Sir" was the reply.

"And how are you getting on?"

"Oh, Sir, we are getting on very well."

"How many natives have you under your orders?"

"Well Sir about 500 on 'em altogether."

"Do you speak their language?"

"No Sir I dont."

"Well then how do you manage to let these natives understand what they are to do?"

"Oh Sir I'll tell you, I tell these chaps three times in good plain English, and then if they dont understand that, I takes the lukri (the stick) and we get on very well."

The ludicrousness of the whole was too much for Sir Bartle's gravity and he & Mr Ellis burst out laughing—and were obliged to turn away.

They discovered that this navvy was a most kind hearted fellow, much loved by the natives under his charge, who would do anything for him.

He of course, when he made the confession, had no idea to whom he was speaking.

Sir Bartle told me this anecdote, with great glee.

To go back to Scinde. My duties & responsibilities increased as I was appointed to the Engineering Charge of a Steam Flotilla which the Railway Coy were establishing on the River Indus, to run between Kotru our Railway terminus and Mooltan, which by the River was 700 miles. These steamers were intended to accommodate the traffic between the Scinde & Punjab Railways until the Indus Valley Railway, proposed by our energetic Chairman Sir W. P. Andrew was made. The Pioneer boat was sent out, built by Scott Russel. She of course came out in pieces—I had to put her together and try her up the River Indus. I laid down "ways" at Kiamari to launch her "broadside on"—a novelty in India, and much scoffed at by many who should have known better. However I built her up complete, Engines & all, and had a most successful launch much to the disgust of the prophesiers of evil. As to the steamer herself, I had always protested against the "lines" on which she was built, as being anything but correct for a river steamer to make passages against a 3 knot current.

She was ordered round to Kotru, and there your Grandmama and I embarked in her to make the trial voyage to Mooltan. Verily it was a weary one, taking 34 days.

I amused myself with my rifle, shooting at crocodiles and alligators—I shot one of the former, over 14 feet in length.

The down trip, with the current, was of course quite easy only occupying 7 days. I had to make considerable alterations in this vessel before I could put her on regular voyages.

She never was a success. Other steamers built by Richardson & Duch followed her & were far better as to speed and accommodation.

While this was going on the Railway was making rapid progress, and was opened in sections. The first traffic Manager appointed by the Railway Co^y. died on his voyage out, so I was obliged for a time to turn Traffic Manager myself, until another was sent out from England.

It was at first thought that it would be difficult to get the natives to travel together in the same carriages on account of caste prejudices, but this proved a delusion. An hour before the time of a train starting, crowds of natives surrounded the booking office clamouring for tickets, and at first there was no keeping them to the inside of the carriages. They clambered up on the roofs of the carriages and I have been obliged to get up on the roofs and whip them off. Females were not allowed to travel in the same carriages as the men. A special carriage was allotted for them and I assure you the noise they made in chattering or rather screaming to one another rendered the identification of their particular carriage quite easy. The men travelling, always carry a roll of bedding with them, and besides they always sat cross legged on the seats, so I took out the seats of the 3rd Class carriages and they then squatted on their bundles on the floor of the carriage and thus economized space. They are very fond of the Railway travelling. One of my Putta-wallahs (liveried messengers) came to me one day saying that he wished to go to his country and asked for the balance of his wages, which he asked me to keep for him. I was very sorry to lose him for he was a very good fellow.

"How long will you be away" asked I.

"Three months" said he. I paid him his wages and with many salaams he disappeared.

About a fortnight afterwards he presented himself and asked to be taken on again, into his old situation. I was astonished to see him as I knew his native place was too far off for him to have visited it and come back again.

"How is this" said I "you cannot have been to your country." He looked confused. I asked him to tell me the truth. After some hesitation he at last told me that he had spent all his money in riding up and down the line smoking his hubble-bubble or water pipe. I could not help laughing at the fellow, so I took him on again.

Just before this occurrence and while we were all very busy in developing the traffic on the Scinde Railway—building and establishing the steamers on the River Indus—Bray, the former Contractor on the line, had entered an action against the Company for £300,000—the damages he said he had incurred by my taking the Contract from him. This sum included something over £176,000 which by the careful account I had kept was the amount, the execution of the Contract works, carried on departmentally, had saved the Company—as compared with the amount it would have had to pay Bray if monied out at his schedule of Contract prices.

The Company required my evidence in England and they also wanted me to select a Staff of Engineers to make the Indus Valley Survey. So one day I received a Telegram, summoning me and also several of my Staff, the important witnesses in the case, to return home to England at once.

This was pleasant news, it came to us early in March 1862 and thus we should avoid the hot season in India, where I had had such hard work—but through which a kind Providence had carried me successfully and in good health.

I regretted most of all the breaking up of my establishment of servants—particularly the loss of my good butler, and Adjun my faithful body servant. It was likely I should be detained in England for 12 months at least. I called my servants together and told them. The butler said he should go home to his Country (Goa) and wait for my return. I knew the General Commanding the Division at Karachi wanted a body servant so I wrote to him recommending Adjun. He at once engaged him. I did the best for the rest of them. I sold all my furniture, horses &c and your dear Grandmama and I set sail for England, leaving your dear Father in charge of some Engineering matters, under Mr Newnham, who was to act for me during my absence.

The voyage home was a pleasant one, cheered with the anticipations of seeing all our dear relatives again after nearly 5 years separation.

You may imagine our delight, when arriving at Charing Cross Station, to find, on the platform, old

Mr Duncan, your Great grand father—who, infirm tho' he was, had travelled all the way up from Scotland to welcome us home. We spent a most happy week together, and then I had to plunge into all the hard work of compiling and arranging the evidence in our defence of Bray's suit—the first sittings in which had just commenced before the Arbitrator.

Very weary was the business, as it dragged its slow length along—but it was the year of the famous '62 Exhibition, and we paid sundry visits there.

Then came the long Vacation, when we had a holiday and went down to Scotland and revelled in the enjoyment of seeing all our dear relatives there, and renewing our acquaintance with many of the old scenes in the Highlands fraught with many happy recollections. But this did not last long. Back to Town and I was again plunged into all the intricacies of the "Bray Case"—which developed itself into larger proportions as we proceeded. In the meantime the Scinde Railway Co^y had decided upon making the survey up the Indus Valley, for the construction of what Mr Andrew rightly termed the "missing link". I was instructed to seek out and form an Engineering Staff for the purpose. While all this was going on I employed my evenings in writing a paper on the "Scinde Railway" for the Institution of Civil Engineers. By working hard at it, I got it completed about January 1863—and submitted it to the Council of the Institution. It was accepted, and read on the evening of the 14th of April that year. The discussion upon it lasted over 2 evenings. The following month I was immensely gratified and proud at receiving a notification that the Council of the Institution had awarded me the first Telford medal and Premium of the year. The gold medal you have probably seen, the 10 guineas worth of books are in my Library—bound and marked as part of the "Telford premium".

It now became clear that the "Bray case" was to be a very very long & protracted one. So the Ry Company decided that I and my Staff of Engineers should go out to India and commence the Survey.

As I was the principal witness on the Defendants side and the Plaintiffs anticipated breaking down my Evidence, they would not agree to my leaving England unless an undertaking were entered into by the R^y Co^y that I should be recalled at any moment that my evidence was required.

This was given, I was free to start—so I collected the Engineers I had selected, 20 in number, and it was arranged that we were to sail in the first week of November. It was a busy time, a run down to Scotland to bid our dear ones good bye again—the purchase of surveying instruments and stationery, and the collecting of the Staff, occupied every hour of my time. At last a special meeting of the Railway Board was held to inspect and take leave of us before our departure. I introduced each Engineer, reported the arrangements I had made, was complimented by the Board and we parted.

VIII

I DESPATCHED the Staff viâ Southampton to
Alexandria, your dear Grandmama & I went to
Marseilles—viâ Paris. It was before the days of
Brindisi. Mr Collins, the eldest of the 1st class
Engineers, was put in charge of the Staff on their
way out to India. He was an Irish man, and not of a
very conciliatory disposition—and great were the
complaints made to me when we foregathered at
Suez. However I threw oil on the troubled waters
and we arrived all right at Bombay. The Staff pro-
ceeded to Karachi by first Steamer; we remained in
Bombay for a fortnight as I had business to settle
with the then Governor, my old friend Sir Bartle
Frere, who received us most kindly, and made
arrangements for our journey up the Indus Valley.
I required and he gave me "purwhanas" to the
Nawabs or Chiefs of the native states thro' which
I thought it probable we should have to pass. He
also said it was necessary that I should be provided
with a police force as my protection and in order to

make a show. The natives not considering that I was any body, if I had not a "tail" to make a display on occasions when I had to visit the chiefs.

My old friend Col. Wilby was then stationed with his Regt., the 4th King's Own, at Poonah—we paid him a visit one day, travelling by rail up the famous Bhore Ghant. We spent a very pleasant day at that beautiful station, and the Colonel told me, of a carriage & fine pair of Arab horses which were for sale cheap. They belonged to Captn Filia Jones who had been British Representative in the Persian Gulf. The horses had been a present to him from the Shah of Persia. On my return to Bombay I immediately went to see the equipage, and after a little bargaining bought the carriage, horses, harness, clothing and groom & coachman's liveries for 2500 Rupees (£250). The Groom and Coachman were only too glad to engage with me—they had excellent characters from Capt. Jones. So there I was, set up with carriage & horses during my stay in Bombay, saving me the hire of such a necessary appendage. When my business with Sir Bartle was concluded I sold the carriage for Rs 600, for I had left my old carriage behind me at Karachi. I took the horses, who, poor things, had been neglected, and were just skin and bone, with us to Karachi on board the Steamer—making a much pleasanter voyage than on the first occasion.

I must however carry you back a little, to the time of our arriving in Bombay Harbour by the P. & O. steamer. Having been kept in England 6 months longer than I had anticipated when I left Karachi, I despaired of collecting around me any of my old tried & faithful servants.

[115]

Well, we were steaming up Bombay Harbour, I was on the poop of the ship, when I saw a figure in the prow of a large boat plying for hire to carry passengers and their luggage from the Steamer to the landing place.

This figure was waving his hat and making great demonstrations, I looked at him more closely, could it possibly be my old Butler? Impossible, for no one in Bombay as far as I was aware, knew of my contemplated return to India at that particular date.

As the boat drew closer to the Steamer, however, I could not be mistaken, there was my old Butler come to meet me. I waved my hand to him. He was quickly on board, and, intensely gratified with my good fortune in thus getting him again into my service, I shook hands with him, handed over to him my bundle of keys, told him how many packages of luggage we had, what hotel we were going to, and all my anxieties on this score were banished. I had again a good faithful head servant, which every where is a great boon, but especially in India when one is travelling about so much.

We arrived in Karachi, and took up our quarters in a Bungalow *at once*. This is easier to do than in England. You have only to give notice to one of the large furniture stores there, where large quantities of second hand furniture are kept, and in a few hours your Bungalow has all the *necessary* furniture for residence, in it. Next morning I was sitting writing when I heard some one enter the room. I looked round—there stood Adjun, making the deepest salaams.

"Halloa, my good fellow how are you? are you still the General's boy?"

"Na Sahib," said he, and he handed me a paper which was from the General, who said that Adjun had been a capital & faithful servant but had come to him that morning and said "General Sahib, my old Sahib has come back—I must go to him again." The General had been so pleased at this exhibition of faithfulness to his old master, that he at once wrote him a splendid "character", while sorry to lose him.

Of course, Adjun, who had thus shown his attachment to me, with which, I confess, I was most gratified, was reinstated as my body servant.

As we were at the beginning of the cold season no time was to be lost in commencing the surveys.

I divided out the whole line, over 600 miles in length, into districts and appointed District and Assistant Engineers to each. Tents, Camels and servants of all kinds were in great demand, but knowing the routine of the thing, I soon got all my Engineers en route for their different localities. My brother Robert was one of my District Engineers and I sent him to that nearest Mooltan—the River Sutlej and Bahawalpoor, which was a very important one. We had to survey four different routes and had a large amount of hard work before us. One of the proposed routes crossed the River Indus at Sukkur, and the practicability of this was a very important question, so I determined to march there myself and investigate all its bearings, in this first cold season's work. So when I had started off all my staff, I organized my camp, and with your dear Ama marched off for Sukkur along the left Bank line of the Indus, so that I could take observations on that, which was one of the routes to be surveyed.

Before starting however I had seen General Cunningham and as he was leaving a large Bungalow he had built for himself, I took it, and transferred all my furniture to it before we started.

On this trip I did not take my escort as I was not likely to be obliged to pass through any independent native state—but I remembered Dr Goodeve's advice and not only took 2 camels load of Soda water with my camp but sent forward supplies to various places on the River Indus, by our Steamers.

We marched up the left Bank route to Sukkur at which place I spent a month in examining and surveying the point where we must cross the Indus if the right bank route from Kotru were decided upon. There were evidently great difficulties in this crossing. One span of 620 feet was a necessity and 2 of 350 & 280 ft respectively. But it was getting very hot, for Sukkur is one of the hottest places in the northern parts of India. So we started back again by the right bank. En route examining what my staff had done during this cold season and withdrawing them back to Karachi to plot their work during the coming hot season. Very glad were we to get within the influences of the cool sea breezes at Karachi.

My new Bungalow was a very spacious one standing in a compound or enclosure of 7 acres on nearly the highest point in the Cantonment, and being two stories in height we caught what cool sea breezes were going.

I took a large office, and my Engineers commenced plotting their cold season's work.

During this hot season I had the pleasure of making the acquaintance of the Hon Col. F. Thesiger (now Lord Chelmsford) whose Regiment was quartered at Karachi. We were very short of ice, all we could get was brought up from Bombay about once a week, and was very expensive. The Col. and I talked this matter over and we wrote to the Wenham Lake Ice Company to know at what price the company would deliver us a cargo of about 800 Tons at Karachi. The reply was that they would do so for a price per ton I now forget, provided we built a proper Ice House to stow it away.

We got up an Ice Company, and I was appointed Engineer to it. I designed an Ice House underground with a branch line off the Railway, which was immediately put in hand under a Contractor who was to finish it before the setting in of the next hot season, and the cargo of Ice was accordingly ordered. I may as well tell you now that when we were daily expecting this cargo to arrive we found out that the vessel had called at Bombay and the ice merchants there, jealous of our establishing an ice house at Karachi and thereby depriving them of our custom had purchased the 800 Tons intended for us at a higher price than we had bargained for, so we were left in the lurch with an empty Ice House on our hands.

But the Col. and I were not to be done, so we purchased an Ice making machine, capable of turning out from 4 to 5 Tons of Ice per day, built a proper house for it at Kotru, and the Railway brought that quantity down to Karachi every night—arriving about 5 o'c in the morning. The rush for it was great and every pound of it was sold at 1½*d*. per lb before 7 o'c. Encouraged by this success we bought a machine for making aerated waters, and commenced the production of Soda water, lemonade &c hitherto manufactured by natives in Kunacher who were by no means particular in selecting good pure water, in fact, it was not to be got in Kunacher, and that was the reason of our establishing our Ice & Soda water works at Kotru on the Indus river. When seen flowing down its natural course the river water looked as much like peasoup as possible. This discolorization arose from fine silt in mechanical suspension.

The mode of clearing it was ingenious and simple. The water was pumped from the river into large tubs. When full the attendant took a piece of Alum between his fingers or fastened to the end of a rod, and past it all over the surface of the water in the tub a few times. This operation caused the formation of a fine film all over the surface of the water, composed of Alum in solution. The specific gravity of this film was slightly greater than that of water, consequently it gradually sank, and in sinking carried down with it all the fine particles of sand and silt which as I said before, were in mechanical suspension in the Indus water. After this operation the water in the tub was left as bright and clear as the finest spring water. Who was the originator of this very simple but effectual filter, I never could discover—but I have adopted it both in other places in India and in England with perfect success for clearing the water used for Engine Boilers. Our Ice Company paid dividends of 15 per cent.

This next cold season's work was to be an arduous one for us all, but for me and your dear Ama especially so. We knew we had to march over 700 miles out & the same distance back again during the 5 months of the cold season. We should have to pass thro' independent native states, so my escort of mounted and foot police had to be organized consisting of 50 mounted and 50 foot soldiers.

My own servants and tent-pitchers amounted in number to 35—for whom tents & provisions had to be collected with a supply of camels to carry them. Then there were my horses for riding the marches, so altogether when we collected at Hyderabad it formed rather an imposing procession. Before leaving I had learnt the position of an old ruined city, called Brahminabad in the "Great Desert" of Scinde—it lay about 15 or 16 miles from the selected course of the left bank line, away in the Desert of rolling banks of sand. I had been much exercised in my mind how we were to get *ballast* for the line of Railway. If all I heard were true, this ruined city, built of brick, would form a grand quarry for ballast, so I determined to visit it and judge for myself, for we cannot in India any more than in England, trust to hearsay.

There were no proper maps of the country thro' which we were to march; on such sketch maps as I could find, Brahminabad was not shown, all I knew was that such a place existed, and it lay on me to find it. After two or three days march from Hydrabad, an intelligent native said that from this point we had better leave the direct course I was pursuing up the Valley and branch off into the Desert, and he undertook to guide us to Brahminabad. Leaving my main camp till my return from this expedition I took a portion of my escort and with a supply of forage and provisions for a desert march we started, and in a couple of days arrived at the ruins, which in extent exceeded all my anticipations. I found that it was situated on the banks of a deserted river bed. There was the depression along which, in times gone by, the river Indus had flowed—there were the old wharf walls. The ancient city had consisted of 3 portions, the largest, surrounded by a wall of solid brick work 20 feet thick and 14 feet high had been the manufacturing or commercial portion on the westerly bank. On the east bank were the Royal palace, and that which I concluded to be the residence of courtiers and the nobility of those ancient days—for without doubt this city, before its destruction, was the residence of the ruling Amir, and of great importance commercially & socially. The native legend is that it was destroyed by an earthquake or some great disturbance some 1000 years ago which broke open a passage for the Indus thro' the rock between Sukkur and Rohri and so diverted its course that the whole of the then cultivated district round Brahminabad became a desert. My careful examination of the ruined and closely crowded houses of the commercial portion of the city confirmed the story of the earthquake.

I found human skeletons buried under fallen doorways, probably arched. I cleared one room of the debris and found in the corner of it a large earthenware vessel on brick supports, under it were charcoal and ashes, and in it the sediment of a charge of indigo solution, close by, the skeleton of the unfortunate dyer, no doubt killed in the midst of his industrial occupation.

In wandering amongst the ruins, speculating upon the probable fate of the large population of this city, I came upon a native, a miserable specimen of humanity, taking some bricks from a wall and loading an attenuated donkey.

I stood and watched him for a short time as he pulled away the bricks from the wall. I then perceived that he had uncovered a hole in the solid wall. I immediately looked down into it and perceived an earthenware chatti in the hole; I at once laid hold of it, and found it contained coins—no doubt the hidden treasure of some ancient inhabitant. I gave the old fellow a rupee with which he was so delighted that unloading his donkey he went off with his treasure, as I did with mine for examination of its contents. I found at least a hatful of old copper coins, of course much oxidised. The majority were "dams" the smallest known Indian coin. In another room I found the debris of a lapidary—some cut portions of which with the coins I brought away with me. I took the latitude and longitude of the city, and afterwards sent the information with a sample of the coins to the Royal Geographical Society.

Convinced that here was a grand quarry for the ballast I wanted—the bricks of which the whole city had been built being hard and well burnt, and our provisions beginning to run short—I marched back to my main camp, much interested with the results of my excursion.

I still keep a number of these coins and bits of dressed carnelian amongst my curiosities.

We proceeded on our march up the Valley of the Indus—passing thro' the territory of Shere Ali Khan who was on friendly terms with the Indian Government and being absent, had sent to the Gov^t. his approval of the line passing thro' his country.

At Sukkur I again had an examination of the Earthquake-rent rocks through which the Indus passes, rendered more interesting from what I had learnt at Brahminabad. In ages gone by, the course of the Indus was round by Jacobabad, it then appears to have passed by Brahminabad and then thro' this Earthquake breach at Sukkur, which meanderings would not surprise you if you saw the vast sandy level plain of the Valley.

A small river Steamer had been ordered up the River Indus, and then up the river Sutlej to meet me near the city of Bahawalpoor for the purpose of ascertaining the best place for crossing the Sutlej or Gharra River. The Steamer took up a complete set of boring tackle, and men accustomed to use it. While this Steamer was making its way up the River we were marching on up the valley. The natives of this region have an idea that all English Sahibs are doctors, and can cure all diseases. Of course I was one in their estimation and crowds of the natives thronged around my camp bringing their sick on charpoys or stretchers expecting me to cure them. The halt, the lame and the blind were there; how I wished that I could heal them all. The principal part of the applicants however were suffering from fever and ague, the result of living in malarious districts. The Government had supplied me, in all my excursions with a large Medicine

Chest, and a considerable quantity of quinine, the potent remedy for the fever which is so prevalent in the Valley of the Indus. My Railway business was pressing so I had to issue an order that I could not attend to any of the sick until 4 o'c in the afternoon; but from early morning each day there they were, so I had to post a cordon of Sentries round my Camp to keep the crowd off. At 4 p.m. a small umbrella tent was pitched in an open place, to which the sacred medicine chest was carried with a chair and table, and a supply of empty wine and beer bottles. I then made my appearance, taking the precaution to put on a special suit of clothes which could be washed & disinfected after the sederunt, for I did not know what cases of an infectious nature might be brought. One by one they were admitted within the line of sentries—and my moonshee standing by my side, explained the questions and answers, which of course passed in each case between the *doctor* and his patient.

I was dispenser too, so that a couple of hours of busy work followed. Mothers sometimes brought their little black naked babies, so burning with fever that it startled one to touch them. An homæopathic dose of aconite, was the sovereign remedy in these cases, and I have seen little creatures whom I had treated the night before running about all well next morning.

Doses of quinine sent the fever and ague adult patients away happy. But the aged were there on stretchers, many of them stone blind—what could I do in such cases? A dose of some harmless drug and a few kind words were all I could give them, poor fellows, but they seemed quite pleased, clutching the bottle evidently believing that they would soon be all right again.

One day my Moonshee came to my tent and told me that there had arrived a rich Zemindar of the district with a considerable train of attendants, who was ill and begged my advice.

He was a man of such position, as the Moonshee explained, that I could receive him in my tent and ask him to be seated. So I agreed to hold the consultation in my tent. He entered having of course taken off his shoes.

I motioned him to a seat. I found he was very ill suffering from fever and ague. Quinine of course was the remedy—but unfortunately my stock was running very low, and I was bound to keep sufficient for my own staff of attendants and followers. I hesitated for a while, pondering what was best to be done.

I daresay my patient thought that I was deeply studying his case. I determined to try what *faith* in a dose would do. So I called for an empty beer bottle, washed it out with water from my patients koojah—for the natives will not drink water drawn by any one but themselves or their own people. I then put into the bottle a table-spoonful of Carbonate of Soda, filled it with water from his koojah and told my patient to take a tablespoonful night and morning! With many salaams and thanks he left me and returned home. Three days afterwards when I had marched on up the Valley at least 30 miles, I saw a cavalcade approaching my camp. It arrived and my Moonshee told me it was this Zemindar who had come to tell me that my medicine had quite cured him and he had brought some presents for my acceptance.

I interviewed him, he was profuse in his thanks and I found from his pulse that the fever had left him. So here was undoubtedly the result of faith in the medicine he was taking which he had every reason to believe was quinine.

His present consisted of a large quantity of fruits, principally oranges, and large baskets of sweeties of various kinds; the sweets did not look at all inviting, but the oranges were most delicious and acceptable.

IX

DEALINGS WITH THE NAWAB OF BAHAWALPOOR—THE
STATE VISIT—CROSS LEGGED DIGNITY—AN AVENUE OF
HORSES—THE RECEPTION—MISUNDERSTANDING ABOUT A
BAROMETER—THE SIGHTS OF BAHAWALPOOR—MOOLTAN
AND LAHORE—WINES FOR THE NAWAB—DOSE FOR IN-
TOXICATION—HIS HIGHNESS COMES ON BOARD—MIS-
GIVINGS OF GUILTY ROYALTY—A DRUNKEN EXIT—
POISONED AT LAST.

BUT now I am approaching the boundary of the
Territory of the Nawab of Bahawalpoor, an in-
dependant native state of considerable extent,
through which it was necessary that the Indus Valley
Railway should pass. At this time the Nawab was
in disgrace with our Indian Government on account
of his tyranny and grievous cruelty to his subjects.
He had lately seized a native of his State who for
years had been resident at Mooltan in the Punjab,
and become naturalized there. He was a merchant
—had made money—and one day crossed the river
Sutlej into Bahawalpoor to look after some little property he had there. The Nawab at once seized him
& demanded a large sum of money from him. On
a refusal the cruel tyrant ordered his ears and nose
to be cut off—which order was at once obeyed. Our
Indian Government had sent a very strong remonstrance, and there was a party in the State most
anxious for the displacement of their oppressor, and
the establishment of British rule.

Such was the state of matters when I encamped on the borders of Bahawalpoor state—through which very few Englishmen had ever travelled, and certainly no white lady. It made us somewhat nervous I confess. Trusting however that we were in the hands of a kind overuling Providence, that our path of duty was plain, that I had a faithful lot of servants and soldiers as my "following", I despatched my Government Perwannah to the Nawab, and awaited his reply and permission to march through his state.

A few days elapsed which I employed in examining the country on the Scinde side of the border, and shooting wild fowl as a change from the constant jungle mutton, when one morning a cavalcade appeared—it was one of the Nawab's Viziers, or Ministers bearing the Nawab's gracious permission to enter his territory and appointing the Vizier to accompany me and see to our safety.

Of course I had to accommodate him with a tent while with my camp, and next day we started. We had at least 8 days marching through the State before we reached the city of Bahawalpoor where the Nawab's palace was situated.

The excitement we created was great—crowds surrounding my camp to get a peep at a white lady, and to see what English ways were. This curiosity was mostly evident amongst the native women. My guard on these occasions was most useful, indeed I could not have got on without them.

The City of Bahawalpoor lies about 2 miles from the Banks of the Sutlej river, and I selected a site for my camp about halfway between them, for the convenience of communication with my Steamer which arrived soon after I had pitched my camp— and was another object of native curiosity. In marching through the Bahawalpoor State, we were regaled every night by the growls of tigers. They were protected by the Nawab as he allowed no one to hunt or shoot them but himself. I had to have a complete circle of fires lighted all round my Camp, for my horses and those of my mounted guard formed a great attraction. As I had a Vizier in my camp I could not even propose to have a shot at them.

He proposed that after the grand dhurbar, at which the Nawab was to receive me—a tiger hunt *might* be organized in my honour. I may as well say here that it never came off—I was far too busy.

As soon as my camp was organized, I started in my steamer on the River in search of the best place for a Railway to cross. Of course I took my attendant Vizier with me, who was profoundly astonished at all he saw on board—never having seen one before, and being utterly ignorant of the power of Steam and the mode of applying it.

In a few days I got notice that the Nawab would receive me at his Palace in Grand dhurbar, & appointing the day and hour. His Highness's carriage was to fetch me. I then began to realise that I must take him a present. Unfortunately I had forgotten this important part of such a reception before starting. I overhauled my possessions and selected from them, very reluctantly, a binocular glass, a six chamber revolver (one of a brace I had), a rifle and, what I regretted to part with most, an aneroid Barometer, for the pocket, in an aluminium casing. The day arrived and, at the appointed hour, the Nawab's carriage drew up opposite my tent. It was a most astounding vehicle drawn by 4 Arab Horses a groom at the Head of each. Imagine a 4 post bedstead on 4 wheels painted red, yellow and all gaudy colours; the 4 posts supporting a lofty canopy hung round with gaudy festoons having deep gold fringe. On the mattress or bed, which was covered with a shawl of fine Indian needle work was a large pillow covered in the same way. Upon this I was to sit cross legged. But how I was to get into this position with any sort of grace or dignity was the difficulty.

My bodyguard of infantry and cavalry men all drawn up in proper form ready to close round the carriage on my taking my seat and form my escort. A crowd of natives had assembled as well as all my own people. Your dear Ama and I had a good laugh, for it was indeed a ludicrous position to be in; but it had to be faced and with the best grace I could command, and assisted by the Vizier I mounted, crossed my legs as well as I could, and we started. As the carriage was without springs and the roads simply awful, you may imagine that I had a very uneasy ride, but consider the dignity of the thing! Through the miserable narrow streets of the city we passed at a slow pace for the crowd was great and had to be driven back in many cases (I am sorry to think) by blows inflicted on them by the Nawab's soldiers and police who also were in attendance. At last we arrived at the entrance to the Palace grounds where I was to alight. From this entrance was a straight path up to the Hall in which the Dhurbar was to be held. On each side of this path were drawn up all the Nawab's stud of Arab Horses, each with a groom at his head, and cloathed with

[131]   9-2

magnificent horse clothes, their hoofs painted with red and yellow paint. It was a curious sight.

Between this assemblage of horses I walked solemnly up, the Vizier by my side and followed by my Moonshee and one of my people carrying the presents. The reception hall was crowded with the Nawab's ministers and officials. At the far end was the Nawab himself seated cross legged upon the Musnud, a large cushion. In the front of the Musnud was a large square carpet beautifully embroidered, on each side margin of which stood the officers of state according to their rank, but none standing on the carpet. The Nawab was dressed in a robe of cloth of gold, on his head an indescribable covering, something between a cocked hat and a mitre, also covered with cloth of gold but studded with magnificent jewels of all kinds.

As I entered the doorway of the Hall, of course I uncovered and halting made a very low bow. The Nawab rose and held out his hand as he came to the edge of the aforesaid carpet. I approached him as he stood there—he held out his hand and grasping mine led me forward and seated me on his right hand on the Musnud, where I was obliged again to sit cross-legged, any thing but a dignified attitude. But here I must describe the appearance of my host.

He certainly was not four and a half feet high—his complexion copper-coloured, his hair black and well oiled, his features by no means bad, but the expression any thing but pleasing. Through my Moonshee he welcomed me to his country, and I replied in the most courteous sentences I could put together. I then begged his acceptance of, first the revolver which he handled in rather an awkward manner, I dont think he had ever seen one before, certainly not a six chambered one; then came the rifle which he seemed to understand better—then the binocular glass which puzzled him somewhat— and last of all the aneroid barometer, which undoubtedly was a novelty to him. In presenting it I explained its uses, how it would tell him if the weather would be propitious for his hunting parties and so on. He listened and smiled and nodded, as if he perfectly understood my elaborate description. I then opened my business with him and he replied giving us permission to survey for and construct a line of Railway through his State. This was all I wanted to obtain, and as I was by this time cramped and weary of sitting cross-legged, I asked permission to retire, which was graciously granted, and backing out from his presence I returned to the entrance gate, where my escort, and the before mentioned carriage were awaiting me. Of this carriage with its bumps and discomfort, I had had quite enough so I dispensed with it and mounting my own beautiful white Arab, which was also in attendance, I rode back to my Camp at the head of my own escort, quite satisfied with the result of my day's work, and much amused with all I had seen. While I was describing it to your Ama, in rushed the Nawab's grand Vizier, saying that the Nawab sent his best salaams, but I had forgotten to leave the key to wind up the gold watch! Alas what a blow was this to my conceit of having delivered a clear description of the construction and uses of an Aneroid Barometer.

The Grand Vizier then told me that the Nawab had seen my white Arab, and should like me to add that to my other presents. I told him at once that I could not do so, as it was my riding horse which I could not replace so far from home. You may guess what were my inward thoughts as to the impudence and what we should call bad taste of such a demand. To smooth matters a little, I asked the Vizier what really would be, next to my horse, the most acceptable present I could make to His Highness. Very confidentially he replied that the Nawab was very fond of Wine and Spirits. I told him I quite understood and that on my return journey from Mooltan & Lahore I certainly would bring him a present of this kind. The Grand Vizier then said that His Highness was desirous that my wife and I should see all that was worth seeing in his city, and it was arranged that on the following day we were to ride on horseback to see all that was to be seen. I declined the offer of the carriage again.

Next day, attended by the Grand Vizier & my special Vizier we started, followed of course by my cavalry Escort. All the inhabitants men women and children turned out to see us; the white lady, on horseback too, was the great attraction.

The *mint* (no less) was to be the first curiosity to be shown us.

Through miserable unpaved streets we passed— they were very narrow, and crowded with natives— so our progress was slow and dignified.

On one side of one of the narrowest streets, there was for a short distance a fence composed of common matting fixed to Bamboos driven into the ground, and about 7 feet high, here we were halted and requested to alight. A breadth of the above mentioned matting was drawn aside and we were invited to enter, which we did and found ourselves within a small enclosure perhaps 15 yards square, at one end was a shed also of mats and bamboos, in the middle of which our conductors pointed out the projecting end of the trunk of a tree, which had been driven endwise in the ground. In the centre of the projecting end, about 18 Inches from the surface of the ground was a piece of metal driven into the wood, on examination I perceived that this was engraved and formed the die or mould for *one* face of the piece of silver to be coined.

Of course it was useless unless the die for the other face of the Coin was available. This upper die stamp was most carefully kept by the Nawab's officers—but was produced to show me the process of coining. Thus it was managed, a small piece of pure soft silver hammered flat was carefully weighed and roughly clipped until it was of the accurate weight of the coin to be stamped. The piece was then laid upon the face of the lower die. The upper die was held upon it by a roughly made pair of tongs, and a native struck it with a heavy sledge hammer. One good blow was sufficient, the coin being of soft silver was stamped on both faces and was ready for circulation. No accurate roundness, no finish of any kind—just the impression of a few Arabic letters. Can you imagine any thing more primitive, rude and barbarous?

Such was the Bahawalpoor Mint. We again mounted and were paraded all through the filthy slums of the city. Grand or even moderately impressive buildings they have none. But there is a large native population, how they live I could not tell you—their appearance was anything but pleasant. Their Nawab was not popular—he was a cruel tyrant.

One anecdote of him was told me. He had issued an order that if any of the land cultivators saw a tiger in the jungles, he was at once to inform the Nawab's officers specifying the exact spot where the tiger was to be found. Just before I had arrived in his state, an unfortunate farmer had spotted a tiger and had given the requisite notice. Next day in great state the Nawab proceeded to the place but no tiger was to be found, he had shifted his quarters during the night.

The unhappy farmer was called up and there and then his ears and nose were cut off. Fancy such injustice and cruelty? Many of the inhabitants thought that I was an Emissary from the Indian Government sent to endeavour to redress their grievances—and deputations came to me, during the night to ask me, what success was attending my interference in their behalf. Of course I was obliged positively to disown any thing like a political Mission, much as I sympathized with them. Evidently the Nawab knew his danger, for the water he had to drink was brought daily in special sealed jars which had been filled across at the Sutlej river in British territory.

The mention of the Sutlej reminds me that I had fixed upon the best place for crossing that river for the Railway and had set my people to work to put down borings in the river to ascertain how deep we should have to go for proper foundations. Leaving

my brother Robert (your grand Uncle) in charge of
this work and the survey of the line in the im-
mediate neighbourhood of Bahawalpoor City, we
crossed the river in my steamer and proceeded in our
march 120 miles to Mooltan, where the Indus
Valley Section was to join the Punjab line of Railway, then open to Lahore & Amritzur. Through a
flat, well cultivated country we marched—no
Engineering difficulties presenting themselves, but
all the inhabitants looking most anxiously forward
for the completion of a Railway which would enable
them to send their produce to market. We arrived
at Mooltan and encamped in a very pleasant place
near the City.

We were very hospitably and kindly received by
such Government officials as were not out in the
Districts, and we spent a very pleasant week there
while I was inspecting the approaches to the existing
Railway Station & fixing on the line we were to take.
It was necessary that I should see Sir Donald
McLeod who was then Lt Governor of the Punjab
and who was at Lahore—so leaving my Camp in
charge of my escort, who were glad of the rest, we
started by rail for Lahore. On our arrival Sir
Donald sent us a nice open carriage and four horses,
which he said he placed at our disposal during our
stay. This was a very kind considerate action on his
part, for the hire of any vehicle in Lahore was
exorbitant.

Of course I waited on Sir Donald and our business
arrangements were satisfactorily settled in a short
time. There was much to see at Lahore, it is a very
fine City with beautiful buildings, fine public
gardens and manufactories of Indian needlework

and weaving—all of which were most interesting, particularly after our weary march of over 600 miles through the Jungles. We visited the large City of Amritzur where we saw much that was entertaining and instructive—we saw the manufacture of the famous Indian Shawls and other wonderful needlework productions. But our stay was limited, for we had to march all that 600 miles back again, and I had to inspect all the work of my Engineering Staff en route; quite as much as we could manage before the hot weather set in.

Not forgetting my promise of a present of wine and spirits, to the Nawab of Bahawalpoor, I purchased a lot of Champagne, Port, Brandy &c, and bidding adieu to kind Sir Donald and many other kind friends, we left for Mooltan and once more started camp life again.

Marching quickly to the Sutlej my Steamer again took us across, and my Camp was pitched in its old place. I found that the borings in the river were completed, and that my Brother had got well on with his survey. I sent my present to the Nawab with all proper salaams.

The following day to my astonishment a bullock cart came up to my tent and with it was the Grand Vizier—on the cart were all the cases of wine & spirits which had formed my present to His Highness. With many salaams the Vizier entered my tent, and informed me that His Highness was exceedingly obliged for the present, but it would be an additional obligation if I would label each bottle, telling him how much would make him drunk? I was much amused, while I could not but be horrified at such a request, as I have no doubt you will be when you read this.

There was nothing else for it, it must be done; so your dear Ama and I set to work that evening and labelled the bottles—giving him moderate doses! In the morning the bottles were sent back to the Palace. In return the Nawab sent a lot of silk shawls & silk of native manufacture as a present to us.

You will recollect that I told you of my having taken my attendant Vizier one or two trips on the river in my little Steamer. While I had been absent at Mooltan he had told the Nawab of the wonderful things he had seen in these trips, no doubt exaggerating every thing in the flowery manner common amongst Eastern nations.

The result was, I received a message from His Highness asking me to give him a trip in the Steamer —as he had never *seen* one. I replied that I should be happy to comply with the request but I had no appliances on board to enable me to receive His Highness in a fitting and proper manner. This I hoped would stop him, but no. The reply came that proper appliances should be sent down to the Steamer from the Palace.

I could not get off this troublesome business. I sent word that 3 P.M. the next day, must be the time for the embarkation, and as the Steamer was small I could only admit 20 of his followers on board. They told me the Nawab was coming on horse back.

Next morning His Highnesses people were seen hurrying down to the landing place where the

Steamer was moored to the Bank carrying fine Carpets and one specially decorated gilt chair, which was to be the substitute for the Musnud on this occasion.

My camp, rather an extensive one, was pitched near the sort of pathway which led from the city down to the landing place a distance of about $2\frac{1}{2}$ miles. This pathway led across several *nullahs*, channels like canals, which in the rainy season and when the river was flooded were full of water, but then dry. The road or jungle track was taken across these nullahs diagonally, so as to make the descent to the bottom of the nullah and the ascent on the opposite side as easy as might be. As my narrative proceeds you will perceive the reason for my describing these very nasty places on the way to the Steamer.

As the hour approached, I sent your Ama down to the Steamer with a small foot police escort who were to go on board. My mounted escort and the rest of the infantry were drawn up in line opposite my tents. My own horse, an old cavalry charger stood at my tent door, ready for me to mount on the approach of the Nawab. By and bye we saw a great cloud of dust and heard a tremendous tom toming approaching through the jungle.

I mounted and took up my position in the front of my troops. The cloud of dust still came on—and we saw two enormous flags in the middle of it. As it approached we saw between the flags the Nawab, not on horseback but on the box seat of a small Victoria carriage driving or making pretence of driving four fat Arab horses each being led by its syce or groom. The carriage was painted red & yellow in the most barbarous fashion, and was empty. This formed the central group; on each flank marched His Highnesses army in line extending from flank to flank at least a quarter of a mile. Any thing more ludicrous I never saw.

My charger seemed to consider the approach of such a noisy party as dangerous. He became very restless and at last reared, swung round and in spite of all my endeavours to stop him galloped off into the jungle. My troopers seeing me gallop off in this way thought it their duty to follow, making the matter still more absurd and ludicrous. Making a short detour I soon brought my refractory steed under command again and came, with my following, at a smart gallop back to the point of reception, where the Nawab had brought his vehicle to a stand. The grand Vizier came forward and delivered a message from His Highness, requesting that I would take a seat along side of him on the box of his carriage. To have refused such an invitation from Royalty, such as it was, would have been rude, so I felt myself forced to accept it, though with many misgivings as to what would befall us in passing the nullahs I described to you, and making the Nawab a low bow, took my seat alongside him. Beside the grooms who *led* the Horses, supposed to be driven by His Highness, there were walking on each side the carriage about a dozen natives in Royal livery, who kept quite close to it.

Their use did not appear till we arrived at the first nullah and commenced the descent—when the carriage heeled over so much that it would have fallen on its side but for these attendants.

Those on the lower side put their shoulders to the side of the carriage, while on the upper side their comrades hung their whole weight on it, and so balanced matters that we did not topple over.

Ascending on the opposite side of the nullah this operation was reversed. But imagine the position of those on the box seat. First the Nawab high above me, then I above the Nawab—both of us clinging for our lives to the rails of the seat.

You will say how could the Nawab hold on with the reins in one hand and his whip in the other; well this was managed as regards the whip by a special servant told off for the purpose who solemnly carried it throughout the drive—as to the reins they were not in use, and gave His Highness no trouble.

Nor were they to be relied on, for an extra pull coming on one of the leaders reins it broke. We stopped and the rein was tied in a knot just in front of one of the terrets through which it passed, and consequently could be of no practical use for guiding the team. All this was going on while the army on each flank was struggling and forcing their way through the high grass jungle the innumerable tom-toms, or small kettle drums, were being vigorously beaten and creating a fearful noise. At last we arrived alongside the Steamer, from which to the bank were placed two or three planks. I escorted the Nawab across them and led him to his chair of State on the quarter deck. While doing this there was a rush of his attendants to get on board and I saw that it would be necessary to stop it or we should have the deck uncomfortably crowded. I asked the Grand Vizier to order that no more should come on board. His order had no effect the crowd still pressed on, so as a last resource I ordered my followers to pull away the planks, which they did at once and into the river fell those who were on them. There was no danger of their being drowned for all the natives swim like fishes. They all scrambled out looking very foolish.

I gave the order to start, when there was a shout raised that the two little princes, children of the Nawab, were not on board. The planks were again laid to the bank and the two Ayahs carrying the two little princes came on board. These children appeared to be about 6 and 8 years old respectively. They like their father were gorgeously dressed. The ayahs, or nurses were both very fine looking women.

More about them by & bye.

As our course was up stream, our speed on board the Steamer was slow and the Army did its best to keep pace with us along the banks of the river and still thro' high grass.

The Nawab seated in his gilt chair, seemed quite pleased. We came to a broader part of the river and I gave orders to put about and run down stream. This was done, and of course the speed of the Steamer increased so much that the Army on the banks had no chance with us.

Immediately there arose a cry from the banks "*Legya, Legya!* They are taking him away, They are taking him away." A suspicion that this was true dawned on the mind of the Nawab and he became furious—he drew his dagger and flourished it

about—ordered all his attendants to draw their
swords and foaming at the mouth demanded to be
put on shore again. I sat still and through the
Moonshee kept assuring him that all was right and
that by & bye I would take him back to the landing
place. Abject terror seemed to have taken hold of
him. His conscience no doubt accusing him of the
many atrocities he had committed which quite
merited punishment and dethronement at the hands
of his subjects—besides some severe action on the
part of the Indian Government.

Here perhaps it had arrived, and he was in my
power. I saw all this and I smiled and said all I could
to calm him, but nothing would do it, till I ordered
the steamer about again, and we commenced our
return voyage, on perceiving which the daggers and
swords were resheathed—and the Nawab ordered
his hubble-bubble or water pipe and some strong
drink. What that drink was I do not know—but by
the time we arrived at the landing place again His
Highness was helplessly drunk, and was threatening
all sorts of things.

I requested his attendants to take him ashore but
they were so frightened of the little wretch that they
dare not touch him. So at last I just took hold of him
round the waist and all but carried him ashore,
handing him over to some of his people who actually
carted him away in a bullock gharrie, gold garments,
jewelled headgear and all.

Was it not a pitiable sight? I may as well here
anticipate a little. I told you that 2 Ayahs and 2
little Princes were on board the Steamer, well about
3 months after the above occurrences, the Ayah of

the younger of the two princes, instigated by his oppressed subjects, poisoned the Nawab, but what was worse, poisoned the elder prince, in order to bring her pet prince on to the Musnud.

When this happened our Indian Government stepped in, appointed an English officer as Regent—took the young prince under its care, gave him a first class education, and he now occupies the Musnud of Bahawalpoor. I am told that he by no means follows in his father's footsteps.

X

A GREAT FLOOD IN KARACHI—SAVING THE BUNGALOW—A
DIGRESSION ON THE VOLUNTEER CORPS—A BULLET
THROUGH A HAT—VOLUNTEERS *v.* LINE REGIMENTS—AN
EXCITING SHOOTING MATCH—RETURN TO ENGLAND—THE
BRAY CASE CONCLUDED—CIVIL ENGINEER IN ENGLAND—
A NARROW ESCAPE IN A COAL MINE—THE BRUNTON
TRAMWAY SYSTEM.

THE day after the above adventure on the
River, we commenced again our return
march, glad to be quit of the attentions of
Royalty such as we had experienced. The whole of
the distance to Hydrabad & Kotru, I had to inspect
the portions of the line surveyed by my Staff; nothing worth recording here occurred to us, and
weary of jungle life, thankful to a kind Providence
that had watched over us & brought us back in
health and safety, we arrived at our comfortable
Bungalow at Karachi.

We had marched 600 miles out and the same
distance back in 5 months.

The Frere Hall was then being built and I was an
active member of the building Committee. It was
making good progress. During the ensuing hot
season all the surveys then made were plotted and
checked—good progress was found to have been
made.

In the month of August of this year 1865 an un-usual fall of rain took place, 20 Inches of rain fell within 6 hours—causing great damage over a district extending about 25 miles round Karachi. The flood which came down the river Mullur was of unprecedented height. On a rising ground up that valley was a village to which during the Monsoon rains, the inhabitants of the neighbourhood were accustomed to retire with their flocks, camels, &c. This had been their custom for time out of mind, and here they concluded they were safe. They erected a large number of mat huts, for they numbered some 150 different families. On the occasion of this flood, the whole of these unfortunate people were suddenly caught by it and swept away down the river to the sea.

Some distance below this village there was a Railway Viaduct crossing the river. I had built it of such height that the lower edge of the girders was 3 feet higher than the level of the surrounding flat country on each side of the river. The viaduct was of great length—having 21 spans 80 feet each.

When the flood had risen to the bottom of the girders, down came the wreck of the above men-tioned village. Mats, bodies of human beings, camels, sheep &c became piled against the girders of the viaduct, forming a regular barrier to the flood which rose and went clear over the top of them, causing such a lateral pressure that 9 spans at least gave way and were pushed off the piers.

Such was the force of the torrent that 2 of the iron spans, though weighing 60 Tons each, were carried nearly 2 miles down the river.

Of all the inhabitants of this unlucky village only one man escaped. He saved himself by clinging to the tail of a dead camel. He was carried out to sea, and ultimately was washed ashore not far from Karachi.

But what think you we in Karachi were suffering, while this misfortune was taking place. Most of the Bungalows there & all the houses in the native town are built with sun dried brick—that is muddy clay, moulded into the shape of a brick and dried in the sun.

As you may suppose such walls if exposed to violent rain would become quite soft, returning to their original mud, and would fall down.

Such was the case on this memorable occasion and 800 houses succumbed in Karachi.

The better class of Bungalows, of which mine was one, are built of stone not set in Mortar as they should be, but in that selfsame mud, while the lower floors are just formed of the same, smoothed down flat, and allowed to dry and harden sufficiently to bear walking on.

Then to add to this, the roofs are formed of loose tiles, constantly displaced by the crows and in case of rain leaking fearfully. Imagine the misery and anxiety your dear Ama and I were in, on that memorable occasion, the former very unwell and unable to leave her bed, on which the rain was pouring down from the roof.

I kept shifting the position of her bed, but there was no escaping the deluge from the roof. At last I placed her in one of our camp beds with frame for mosquito curtains over which I placed a waterproof sheet. But what was going on downstairs all this time? My servants were calling out that the dining and drawing rooms were flooded. I rushed down and found that the foundations of the walls of the Bungalow were in danger.

I sunk a large hole in the floor of the drawing room to collect the water and then put all my servants to work to bale it out with buckets, throwing the water clear of the outer walls. In this way I believe I saved my Bungalow from sharing the fate of that of the chief Royal Engineer of the District situated some 300 yards in rear of mine, in which the front wall fell and left the Bungalow like an open dolls house.

Great was the misery occasioned by this visitation but it taught a lesson, and the buildings in Karachi are now being erected in a more substantial manner.

The whole of the Indus valley survey being in a very forward state in fact nearly completed, I wrote out my reports upon it with full details and recommended the adoption of the left bank line. In September 1866 I received a telegram from the Railway Board in England summoning me home, in order to give evidence in the Bray case, which had all this time been dragging on its weary way.

The Indus Valley Engineering Survey Staff was to be broken up. Before this took place we all met in the Government Gardens at Kunachee one morning and a Photograph of the group was taken. This Photograph you have often seen.

I frequently look at it with mingled feelings of pleasure and pain. I recognize many there who had shared with me all the difficulties and hardships of jungle life, and had shown themselves well worthy of the confidence reposed in their engineering talents and energy, and some of these are gone, passed away from this world of care & trouble to, I trust, a happier home above.

Before leaving, however, I must take you back a long way, even to my first arrival at Karachi during the famous Indian Mutiny, and give you a history of my connexion with the Volunteer Corps which had just been established when I landed.

It was under the command of Captn Goldsmid now General Sir Frederick Goldsmid. I at once offered my services and was enrolled a Captain in the Corps. I used my influence with the members of my Staff and other of the employees of the Railway Company, and I very soon brought in a large number of recruits. Of course your dear Father was one, and he was enrolled as Lieutenant. Practice in rifle shooting and regimental drill was necessary, and as the presence of such a force, in those dangerous times, and their efficiency, were of great importance, regular drills were organized. Sir Bartle Frere assigned the rifle butts at Scandal Point for our rifle practice, and every morning at day-break a squad of the Corps was ordered out. I took great interest and pride in the Volunteer movement, altho' it was held up to ridicule by the Officers of Line Regiments. The constant regular practice soon made my men very fair shots—and by & bye we challenged one of the line regiments to a competition.

It resulted in our Victory. This challenging of the different regiments quartered at Karachi and our invariable success at the trials of skill was kept up for 4 years. On my return to Karachi after the visit to England, I found that our numbers in the Volunteer ranks had greatly increased.

Sir Frederick Goldsmid was leaving Karachi. I was selected to succeed him in command, and I felt very proud of the honour. General Cunningham was then in Military command of the Division and was much annoyed at the repeated victories of the Volunteer Rifle teams, over the different Line Regiments.

He got up a Subscription for prizes at a Rifle Tournament as he called it. This subscription was very handsomely met. The highest prize was 1000 Rupees and there were various others of smaller amount.

My Volunteers diligently kept up their practice. Unfortunately my Engineering duties kept me out in the Districts at the time when the Tournament was to come off. I regretted this the more, for regular morning practice had made me a very good shot and I should have been of use. However the Contest came off and resulted in my store keeper at the Railway works carrying off the first prize.

So here was another blow for the General, and also the Colonels of the Regiments, who competed.

One of these Colonels, I met in the Jungles, as I was returning to Karachi. He was out on a sporting expedition. Taking a walk in the jungles in the evening our conversation turned upon rifle shooting generally—the Colonel arguing that shooting at a target on a rifle range was much easier than shooting at an object in the jungle for instance, and he proposed to put his sun topee on a bush, then and there and he would make a wager that I could not hit it at a distance of 150 yards. I tried to persuade him not to run such a risk of having his fine sun hat destroyed. Nothing would satisfy him but that the shot should be tried. The topee was put in the bush, the distance was stepped out, and because in the dim light the grey topee was not by any means a conspicuous object—the Colonel insisted on putting his white pocket handkerchief over it; I fired and much to his disgust the topee and the handkerchief were utterly spoiled. Here was the result of my regular practice at the targets.

But in spite of being considered egotistical I must tell you a further instance. When we got back to Karachi the General told me that he could not yet be satisfied as to the superiority of the Volunteers as marksmen. He proposed a Sweepstakes amongst all the Officers on the Station including the Volunteer officers of course. In a few days there were 90 entries and the General was convinced in his mind that the tide of victory would turn in favour of the Line, because there were 80 line entries to 10 volunteers. The morning for shooting off this sweepstake trial was fixed. The night before Col. Beville of the Belooch Battalion came to my bungalow, saying he had just arrived and must join in the Match, begging me to lend him a rifle.

This of course I did. At day break next morning there was a tremendous muster at the butts for the whole population seemed interested as well as the garrison.

Col. Beville went ahead of all of us at the short distances, but I was not far behind him.

I was very near to him at the 400 yard range, close to him at the 500 yards and tied with him at the 600 yards. All the other competitors had tailed off. It was a moment of intense excitement both to the Colonel, myself and the assembled multitude. The "tie" was settled to be shot off at the 400 yard range. We tossed up for first shot, the Colonel won —he fired—a bullseye! Great was the cheering. I fired—also a bullseye! Again the Colonel made a bullseye, and so did I.

The cheering and excitement with the noise were any thing but conducive to accurate aim.

At his 3rd shot the Colonel's bullet was just outside the bullseye. My 3rd was a 3rd bullseye thus winning the match for the Volunteers, amid cheers and compliments not easily forgotten. The addition of the 900 Rupees to the Volunteer fund was very acceptable, and we felt ourselves proud of the victory. The Volunteer movement has continued to flourish, and has become established in India in spite of the jeers with which it was at first assailed.

We had now (October 1865) to prepare for our departure for England; that meant the sale of furniture, carriage, horses, tents and stores of all sorts. This unpleasant operation was got through (satisfactorily, as it regards the proceeds) and was followed by what was to me a melancholy duty, that of bidding farewell to so many friends, whose faces, in all human probability we should never see again.

We sailed for Bombay—where we caught a homeward bound P. & O. boat. We had a good passage to Suez—at which place I saw the first vessel enter the new dock there. The Suez Canal was not yet opened. We travelled by rail to Alexandria, and found the Steamer waiting for us. By some gross carelessness the passengers luggage van had been left behind and there were we, starting on a voyage to Marseilles in the month of November, without any clothes but those we were wearing.

Fortunately there were friends of ours on board who lent us some clothing, and when we arrived at Marseilles, we had to purchase a complete refit. *Three* months after we had arrived, in London, the whole of our baggage arrived also. This does not speak much in favour of the management of the Khedive's Railway.

You may imagine our thankfulness and joy at once more setting foot in dear old England & with again embracing your dear Father and for the first time seeing your dear Mother, it was a joyous meeting indeed. I was at once plunged into the intricacies of the Bray case, and it was settled that my examination should proceed. You may imagine the extent and intricacy of the matters in dispute when I tell you that Bray's claim extended over 5700 odd items—every one of which we disputed either as to existence at all, or in quantity or in price.

My examination in chief extended over 2 years and my cross examination over 9 months.

It was a most trying and wearisome business involving such a tax upon my memory and so much reading up. Before it came to an end, I felt thoroughly ill and used up. The result of it all was, what I considered a fearful blunder—a sort of compromise amongst the lawyers, which astonished the Arbitrator as much as it did me.

At the conclusion of this business I determined to commence business as a Civil Engineer and took an office at 13a Great George St. The first business which offered itself was, that I should go down to North Wales and report upon the condition and prospects of the Maenofferen Slate Quarry.

I ought to have mentioned that during the time I was engaged in the Bray case your dear Father obtained an appointment on the Oude and Rohilkhand Railway in India, and he and your dear Mother went thither in 1868 leaving your dear Ama and me grieving much at losing their delightful society. While quartered at Benares in 1869 on the 23 July dear Jack was born, and I became a proud grandfather.

In 1870 your dear Father had been suffering from fever and was ordered home. We were then living at 35 Russell Road and you may imagine with what joy we received and welcomed them back again particularly on finding that the voyage home had restored your dear Father's health. The period of his furlough passed, and although the Railway Co^y were very anxious for his return to India, his health and occasional returns of fever and ague were such, that the Doctors could not recommend him to do so.

My business was increasing and it was decided that he should become my partner.

After my visit to Maenofferen Slate Quarry above mentioned, I made an arrangement with that Co^y. to visit the Quarry one week in every four. The agreement was for seven years—and from the date of that agreement until June 1884 every fourth week, winter and summer has seen me at the Quarry, climbing the mountain side and traversing all the underground workings which are extensive.

In 187–(?) I was appointed Engineer to the Coal Consumers' Cooperative Society which was established at a time when the price of coal had risen to an unprecedented height.

Think of ordinary house coal in London being up to 52/- per ton! My duties were to go down and inspect and report upon the various collieries offered for sale to this Society. They were very numerous and lay in various parts of the country.

Many of them were not in good or safe condition, making it somewhat dangerous to traverse the workings in order to inspect them thoroughly.

I must give you the history of one adventure which occurred on my visit to a Colliery in South Wales. I arrived at the spot early one morning neither the owner nor the head manager was there. I found that the colliery was worked by a long inclined plane driven underground for about half a mile. A steam Engine at the top drawing up the loaded waggons and letting down the empties. I strolled first into the Engine House and noticed that this hauling up of the loaded waggons was done by a *chain* which, since the invention of wire ropes, was altogether prohibited—because the link of a chain breaks suddenly without any warning, while a wire rope always gives signs of weakness before giving way.

I asked the Engine driver when the Government Inspector had been last at the Colliery, he said about a month ago, and he had made a great disturbance about the working with a chain. I told the driver to lower me down the incline very quietly.

I was going down in a waggon with some straw laid upon it. The assistant manager and I were safely landed at the bottom of the incline. For about 4 hours we were wandering through the workings and at last came to the foot of the incline, where I found that to the tail of six loaded waggons which were to be drawn up, they had attached my empty waggon, and were waiting for me to take my seat.

Not if I know it, said I, take off the empty waggon and send word to the Engine Driver to arrange for hauling me up altogether separately from the coals.

This was arranged and the sub-manager and I retired into a deserted tunnel to await the arrival of our conveyance and console ourselves with a pipe.

We had not sat down 2 minutes before we heard a frightful crash. My companion rushed off to see what had happened, and in a short time returned in great consternation—the *chain* had broken, the waggons & coal were in one confused wreck and blocked up the inclined tunnel, which was the only way out of the mine. My first emotion was one of gratitude to our Heavenly Father for having thus guided me in refusing to go up the incline at the tail of this unfortunate train. Had I done so I must have been killed inevitably. By crawling on my hands & knees I succeeded with much difficulty in passing the obstruction and I then on my feet clambered up the remaining length of the incline.

Business now was very brisk, other collieries had to be inspected and my connexion with Maenofferen

Quarry brought me into communication with many other Slate Quarry Proprietors, who wished for reports on their properties; amongst others was the Welsh Slate Quarry, the largest underground Quarry in the world. Your dear father was down there and made a very elaborate survey of the workings with a view to a very large and important removal of the upper strata over a considerable extent of the underground workings and thus prevent a fall of the same. I made an elaborate report on this matter, but circumstances arose which prevented the work being carried out, much to my regret as well as that of the Welsh Slate Coy, for we all foresaw an inevitable fall or collapse. But more respecting this by & bye.

The construction of Tramways in Towns became a popular notion. Companies were formed to make them both in England and on the Continent—we had the Engineership of the Milan and Vercelli Tramways for some considerable time, but eventually retired from them, as we disapproved of the action taken by the native element which got introduced into these Companies. We then saw the importance of an improved system of Tramroad rail, and set our brains to work on the question. The result was the introduction of the "Brunton system" which by simplifying construction has been a success. It has been adopted on the Oxford and Karachi Tramways of which I am the Engineer, and has given much satisfaction   *   *   *

The diary ends here. The following obituary notice is added to the manuscript in another hand.

Obituary. Institution of Civil Engineers
Re John Brunton

JOHN BRUNTON born in Birmingham in the year 1812 began his engineering career as pupil in the works of Messrs Harvey & Co of the Hale Foundry Cornwall. On the expiration of his pupilage he was engaged for two years on the construction of Colliery Railway in South Wales. He was next employed for several years under George & Robert Stephenson on the London & Birmingham Railway & on the Manchester & Leeds Railway. After a brief period of work on the Maryport & Carlisle Line, Mr Brunton practised on his own account in Scotland for four years. He then came south again and carried out work for Messrs Hutchinson & Ritson, contractors in connexion with Railways in Wiltshire, Somersetshire and Dorset.

During the Crimean War he was engaged under T. K. Brunel in the erection of army hospital buildings in Turkey, & in the provision of water supply & landing-piers for them.

In 1857 Mr Brunton was Chief Resident Engineer on the Scinde Railway. The line to be constructed was from Karachi to Kotri a distance of 108 miles & the work was commenced in April 1858 and completed in 1862. In the following year he presented to the Institution an account of the construction of the line, for which he was awarded a Telford premium & Medal. His next work was the survey of the Indus Valley Railway, on the completion of which, he returned to England.

In 1870 Mr Brunton took an office in Westminster, where he practised for 20 years.

During that time he acted as Engineer to some Slate Quarries in Wales and carried out various tramways, & other works.

The last years of his life were spent in retirement at Leamington where he died on the 7th April 1899 at the age of 86.

Mr Brunton during his residence in London frequently attended the meetings of the Institution. He was an Associate on the 3rd of February 1857 & was transferred to the Class of Members on the 21st April of the same year.

Index

East India Railway Co., 82
Edmonton, 36
Ellis, Sir Barrow, 106

Flood (River Mulher), 147
Foot accident, 12
Francis, Smith, Dearman and
Brunton, 3
Freeland, Captain, 60
Frere, Sir Bartle, 91, 98, 104,
106, 114, 150
Frere Hall, 146

Garra, 94
Gharra River, 124
Glasgow, 39
Goanese butler, 88, 116
Golden Horn, 60
Goldsmid, General Sir Frederick, 150
Gooch, Mr Thos. Longridge, 35
Goodeve, Dr, 84, 118
Goolden, Mr Chas., 53
Grand Dhurbar, 130
Great George St, 155
Great Indian Peninsular Railway, 106
Great Western Mill Bay Docks, 45

Haarlem Lake, 11
Harbour case, 9
Harvey and Co., 10
Harvey, Miss, 10
Harvey, Miss Nanny, 10
Harvey, Nicholas, 4, 9, 12
Hawes, Mr, 4
Hayle Foundry Works, 9, 14, 16
Hutchinson and Ritson, 45, 50
Hydrabad, 93, 96, 121, 141

Illium Novum, 68
Indian Mutiny, 83, 85, 150
Indus, 97, 117
Indus Valley Engineering Staff, 149
Indus Valley Railway, 108, 111, 137

Institution of Civil Engineers, 5
Islington, 3, 17
Ivy Bridge, 46

Jacob, General, 98
Jacobabad, 98, 124
Jack, 62, 81, 102, 155
Jarrow, Mr, 83
Jessop, Mr, 1
Jesus College, Oxford, 19

Karachi, 82, 89, 96, 98, 104,
116, 118, 146, 151
Khedive's Railway, 154
Kiamari, 104
Kincaidfield, 45
Kotru, 82, 93, 97, 108, 118,
120, 146
Kunacher, 120, 149

Lahore, 83, 134, 137
Leaden Hall St, 8
Lee Moor Railway, 45
Littleborough Toll, 39
Liverpool and Manchester Railway, 36
London and North-Western
Railway, 12
Louth, Brigadier, 91
Lyons, Lord, 72

Maenofferen Slate Quarry, 155, 158
Manchester and Leeds Railway, 44
Mare, theft of black, 28
Marmora, Sea of, 58
Marseilles, 53, 84
Maryport and Carlisle Railway, 44
Matriculation Examination, 8
McCulloch, 8
McLeod, Sir Donald, 137
Melbourne School, 5
Messagerie Impérial Steamers, 53
Meyers, Dr, 52

INDEX

For EU product safety concerns, contact us at Calle de José Abascal, 56–1°, 28003 Madrid, Spain or eugpsr@cambridge.org.

www.ingramcontent.com/pod-product-compliance
Ingram Content Group UK Ltd.
Pitfield, Milton Keynes, MK11 3LW, UK
UKHW012332130625
459647UK00009B/225